God's Servants: Life lessons from the greatest

By Bill F. Korver

www.metakoi.com

Published by Metakoi Publishing and Lightning Source (a subsidiary of Ingram Content Group), 1246 Heil Quaker Boulevard, La Vergne, TN USA 37086

All Scripture quotations, unless otherwise indicated, are taken from the Holy Bible, New American Standard (NAS) version, copyright by the Lockman Foundation.

Cover Design: Allegra Anne Korver

Interior sketches: Douglas Rowe douglasrowestudios.com

Korver, Bill F.

God's Servants: Life lessons from the greatest

ISBN:978-0-9905783-3-8

1. Christian Service 2. Korver, Bill 3. Biblical biography

Printed in the United States of America

Dedication

This volume is dedicated to three remarkable servants of Jesus Christ. To my parents, Bill & Fran Korver, who served Jesus daily in their home and community. They raised six children to serve Jesus as they modeled what that looked like. No task was "beneath" these two and they performed those tasks skillfully and cheerfully. Together they make a great pair of choice servants of the King, Jesus Christ. They not only modeled service, they regularly taught me and my siblings that serving Jesus was the noblest activity a person could pursue. Their incredible influence on my life cannot be overestimated.

Additionally, my bride, Marcia deserves a great deal of praise. She has faithfully supported me and my feeble attempts to serve Jesus vocationally for more than 35 years. Though extremely talented and gifted in many ways that she could have used in the marketplace, she selflessly poured her life into our three living children and me behind the scenes, out of the limelight, and we are all the better because of her.

For these three, I cannot wait to see how Jesus, the suffering Servant and coming King, rewards them for their multitude of acts of service on that future day when He will reward all His faithful servants!

Acknowledgements

This volume is about those who served God. It details the lives and ministries of seven whose lives are recorded in the Bible. Though I've only read about the seven servants mentioned in this book, I've been privileged to know many others whose lives have greatly and positively impacted my own. My siblings, Bruce, Michelle, Dan, Nancy and Margi, each have modeled service for the King through generous giving, an incredible work ethic, and serving the needy in third world situations and at home. My three living children, Elizabeth, Jared and Allegra each serve others in ways that make me proud and cause me to want to be a better servant.

At Southeastern Bible College, I was privileged to be taught by some choice servants. I am especially grateful for the lives of Dr. Alden Gannett, Dr. John Talley, Dr. James Raiford and Dr. Rick Fairman. These men taught me about the grace of God, how to walk in step with the Spirit, how to proclaim the Word in a way that honors the Savior and coming King, Jesus Christ, and how to rightly interpret the text of Scripture. Dr. Glen Atkins, my Greek professor, was the one who, in a chapel message, planted the seed in my heart for this book.

In vocational ministry, I have been blessed to have many mentors and co-workers who have profoundly influenced me for the better. They include Robert D. Kelso, my first pastor who modeled deep character and a shepherd's heart. Charles R. Swindoll, who modeled grace and encouraged me to be myself, not someone else. Also, Paul Sailhamer, Dave Osborne, Rick Oglesby, and Kevin Wilson have impacted me for the better.

Additionally, I have been immensely blessed by my colleagues at Carolina College of Biblical Studies, professors, staff, Board of Directors and President's Cabinet members, they have taught me much about serving God through their selfless and tireless efforts.

Introduction

For centuries people who follow Christ have been talking and writing about being a servant. There are books on servant-leadership. I've witnessed leaders doing a foot washing service in front of large crowds to demonstrate the concept of serving others.

Many years ago, a godly professor of mine in Bible College spoke in a chapel service about the concept of being a servant. He said, in effect, that God used the words, "My servant..." to personally refer to only a select few people in the entire Bible. Having heard a great deal about being a servant, I thought that was a remarkable fact. To think that of only seven people, in the entire Bible, does God refer to as, "My servant," puts those people in select company. In the interest of full disclosure, God does use the term "My servant" to refer to Nebuchadnezzar, but in the context, it merely means that God is using Nebuchadnezzar to fulfill His purpose, not that Nebuchadnezzar was obeying God from the heart and pursuing God's will. The term "My servant" is also used several times of Jacob, but in those contexts "Jacob" refers to the nation of Israel, not the person who was Abraham's grandson and one of Isaac and Rebekah's twin sons. You may wonder who was called "My Servant" by God? They are all found in the Old Testament scriptures, they are Jesus (though His name is not given in the passage we will consider, he is clearly referred to), Abraham, Moses, Caleb, Job, David, and Isaiah. As a friend of mine is fond of saying, that's high cotton. There are approximately 3200 different people listed by name in the Bible, but only seven of them are described as "My servants" by God. Clearly many more than seven people in all the Bible actively and passionately served God. To be sure, of some it is even said, "Paul is My servant" or some such language. But only of seven people are the precise words, "My servant, Abraham…" (fill in the other six names) used.

Is being named a servant of God kind of like playing the lottery or going to Las Vegas, a matter of luck? No! It is not luck, but something very practical and can be accomplished by any believer in Christ. Other than Jesus, the remaining six examples of servanthood are people with natures like our own. What lessons can we learn from these servants? What can those who serve expect, if anything, from the Master they serve? That is the subject of this book. It is my hope that God will use the truths mined from His Word, the Bible, to transform you and make you more effective in your service for Him. Wouldn't it be great if God were to describe you as "My servant"?!

CONTENTS

Chapter 1

Me, Serve?

Overcoming cultural & personal reluctance

Do you remember being a young child or teenager and being asked by an older person, "What do you want to be when you grow up?" When the questioner asked about what you wanted to be, he was asking: when you get older, what vocation - what career - do you want to pursue? In my day, it was not uncommon for children to respond, "a fireman", or "a policeman", or "a nurse". Occasionally, you might have heard "a professional baseball player" (I grew up in the Mickey Mantle era in his home state of Oklahoma). I suppose if the question were asked these days, the responses might include software developer, website designer or an interior designer.

In my own personal journey, I dreamed of being a baseball pitcher, a history teacher, and an architect all before I completed high school. I never, nor has anyone I have personally known, hoped or said, "my dream is to be a servant". The idea just sounds so humbling, so "beneath" anyone with aspirations. Our culture preaches greatness - you-can-achieve-anything-you-set-your-heart-and-mind-to mindset. The "if you can conceive it, you can achieve it" mentality. Most bow down to the idol of self-image. Having a healthy self-image appears to be in direct opposition to humility and service.

In 1905, an Italian economist named Vilfredo Pareto published some research. He discovered that 20% of Italians owned 80% of all the land in Italy. Conversely the remaining Italians, the 80%, only owned 20% of all the land in Italy. Sometime after Pareto published his findings, others began to study other areas and found Pareto's principle, later to be described as the "80/20 Principle" or the "20/80 Principle", was true in other areas too. As examples, 20% of all hospital patients represent 80% of all visits to doctors/hospitals (some people are chronically ill while others, the majority, are usually healthy). In the judicial system, 20% of criminals commit 80% of all crimes (you've heard the term "repeat offenders"). In technology, software and hardware experts discovered that 80% of all problems are solved by addressing the same 20% of "trouble" issues.

All of this might be well and good, but what does it have to do with God, the Bible, and you? Great questions! The truth is, about 35 to 40 years ago people began to study Pareto's principle as it might relate to the church. Not surprisingly they found that in the average church, 20% of the people did 80% of the financial giving and filled 80% of the ministry positions. Conversely, 80% of the church members only did 20% of the giving and only filled 20% of the serving positions. It is easy conclude that, in the average church setting, some are serving in multiple positions and the giving of very few people carries the church through financially lean times and enables the church to continue its ministry. Two usual results, for the 20% are: 1) they are often exhausted and in need of some relief from the heavy burden of many ministry responsibilities and 2) they often struggle with a sense of bitterness over the many who seem to do nothing to serve Jesus and make their church more vibrant. From the standpoint of the 80%, several issues often arise too: 1) They have remained immature in their understanding of and use of spiritual gifts, 2) they are untrained and/or selfish regarding financial partnership with God through giving and 3) they are often quite demanding, wanting to be served and looking for a "full service" church rather than seeking out service opportunities.

If those statistics hold true at the church you are a part of, imagine the unintended consequences. What would it be like if, rather than 20 % getting involved and giving, 80% or more did? I am quite sure the body of Christ could do much more than it does to demonstrate God's goodness and grace to a world that desperately needs to see it and hear the good news of Christ's death and resurrection, many millions for the first time.

Human nature has not changed since sin became a reality in humanity (Genesis 3). Ever since that terrible choice by Adam and Eve, humans have distorted God's ideals and plan - including their definition of what it means to be great. In Luke's gospel, there is a record of the twelve disciples of Jesus having an argument amongst themselves about greatness - specifically, who among them was the greatest. Each of them concluded that he was the greatest, the other eleven were merely vying for spots #2 - #12. Luke writes the following:

> And there arose also a dispute among then as to which one of them was regarded to be greatest. And He said to them, "The kings of the Gentiles lord it over them; and those who have authority over them are called 'Benefactors.' But not so with you, but let him who is the greatest among you become as the youngest, and the leader as the servant." Luke 22:24-26

Because of that inflated view of self, it is no wonder that they refused to serve. I find it amazing how Jesus responded to their argument. He did not chide them for their desire to be great, He merely corrected their thinking on how one might achieve greatness. Don't you find it refreshing to know that Jesus did not say, "Gentlemen, I want each of you to strive for mediocrity"?

Rather than scolding the desire to be great Jesus applauded the desire. He merely coached them on how to think about greatness. Right thinking about greatness, or any other subject, would result in correct doing about that subject. I see at least three truths Jesus taught in Luke 22:24-26. They are:

1. The tendency for those desiring greatness is to be bossy. "The kings of the Gentiles *lord it over them...*". We tend to be bossy when we get a promotion - a position of authority. If we're not careful we can falsely assume that the measure of greatness is in giving orders to others. The more important and successful we are, the more people we have under our authority. We love moving up the organizational flow chart.

2. We tend to equate titles with success.
Jesus said, "...and those who have authority over them are called 'Benefactors'". There is nothing wrong with titles that go with a position or promotion. Being a CEO, a colonel, or a district manager is not sinful. The problem is when we insist on being addressed by a certain title. I once worked with a man who insisted everyone call him by his title, not his name. Later he earned his doctoral degree and heaven help the man or woman who did not address him as "Dr. _____". I minister in a world of higher education, often a chief offender of this principle. Many who have labored for years to earn advanced degrees insist that others recognize those degrees when being addressed or introduced to others. Know this, titles and degrees earned will never determine greatness.

3. We should voluntarily humble ourselves. Again, Jesus says, "But not so with you, but let him who is the greatest among you *become*

as the youngest, and the leader as the servant"
(Luke 22:26; italics mine). In a culture that honored
the aged, to be a youth, a child, meant to serve the
elderly. Perhaps you've been to a family reunion
where there was an old person who struggled
physically. Usually those who are younger will help
the aged relative to a seat and prepare a plate of
food for them. The younger voluntarily serve the
older. That's part of Jesus' point. We are supposed
to humble ourselves, not humiliate ourselves. I
know a man who, when he was in high school,
thought that to be humble meant to find the most
humiliating thing he could do and do it. What was
his conclusion? He decided the most humiliating
thing he could do was to go around the high school
and scrape up or pick up wads of gum that other
student threw out or spit out anywhere on campus.
He only later discovered that to humble one's self is
not the same as humiliating one's self. He did the
gum patrol to be seen as a servant, not to truly
serve. He came up with a phrase (at least I think it's
original to him), "Humility is not thinking less of

yourself, but thinking of yourself less". A believer in Christ can and should have a healthy, biblical view of self. We are sons and daughter of the Creator and coming King! He has given us talents and spiritual gifts, so all the things we do that please Him are evidence of His grace in and through us. As we choose to think of ourselves less and more about our Lord, the needs that exist around us, and how He wants to use us to minister to the needy, the more we will become like children serving others.

If an Italian economist of a century ago can tell us anything, it is that a great majority of people don't serve. The account from Luke's gospel tells us that Jesus applauded the desire to be great, but He corrected the disciples' erroneous thinking on how that would happen. To truly be great, we need to choose to serve God through obedience to His Word as we minister to others on His behalf.

FOR FURTHER CONSIDERATION

1. Do you find Pareto's "80/20" principle to be true in your church experience?

2. Why do you think most people do not serve? How does this affect those who do serve and the entire church family?

3. Can you recall times when you "lorded it over" others, demanding some title or esteem be given you?

4. What about Jesus' response to the twelve disciples in Luke 22:24-26 is the most surprising to you?

5. How do you think the disciples who heard these words from Jesus felt when He exposed their hearts and gave them a very different message from what they had always heard?

Chapter 2

My Servant, Jesus

God's Ideal Servant

Have you ever worked with a boss who made lots of demands of you and others? Sometimes the demands were not even reasonable - the tasks assigned and the deadlines for completion were impossible! Some people, in fact far too many people, had parents, coaches, or other role models in their lives who taught one thing with their words but another very different thing with their actions.

One of the many things I love and appreciate about Jesus is that He did not merely teach about being a servant (see chapter 1 – Luke 22:24-26) but He also modeled a life of service. Therefore, it is fitting that the first "My Servant" we consider would be the Lord Jesus.

In the days of Isaiah, the prophet of God to Israel, the people of God had wandered far from Him. They were supposed to serve Him as His servants but they are depicted in Isaiah's prophecy as being a deaf, dumb (unable to speak), blind, and disobedient (Isaiah 43:8, 9; 56:10). What terrible adjectives to be described by! Who wants or has use for a servant who does not hear her master's commands? What use is a servant who cannot speak to the master or to others on behalf of the master? Can a servant serve effectively without the ability to see, hardly! Finally, even if they could have heard, spoken and seen, they were disobedient to He who made them and called them to serve Him as their Master. It is in contrast with ancient Israel that God reveals for us His Servant, Jesus. Isaiah 42:1 states, "Behold, My Servant, whom I uphold; My chosen one in whom My soul delights. I have put My Spirit upon Him; He will bring forth justice to the nations." I know of no one who takes the Bible seriously who does not believe that the person described in Isaiah 42:1 as "My Servant" is a reference to Jesus Christ. It may be one the most significant verses in the entire Bible. All of God's Word is inspired (2 Timothy 3:16 and 2 Peter 1:21), but some portions teach truths that are more fundamental and important than others. Why is this verse so significant? It is significant in that it refers to Jesus, but also because it is quoted many times in the New Testament. In Matthew's gospel, when Jesus came out of the baptismal water of the Jordan river, God the Father spoke from heaven in an audible voice saying, "This is My beloved Son, in whom I am well-pleased" (3:17). At first glance it might be missed, but with careful consideration it can be observed that the Father paraphrased the wording of Isaiah 42:1 (when you are the Author of the Book, you can paraphrase it as you wish!). It's not just that the Father quoted the verse, but also the timing of the proclamation He made. Jesus' baptism was the public launching of His ministry. To put it in terms we might identify with, Jesus' baptism was, in some sense, like an ordination service. It was a moment to mark the beginning of

His ministry. Unlike our ordination services, Jesus' ordination council consisted only of His Father - and He passed with flying colors! Later in Jesus' ministry, after calling them to follow Him and pouring His life into twelve disciples, He told them that some of them would not die until they got a glimpse of the glory of His kingdom. A few days later He took Peter, James, and John, the so called "inner circle", up to a mountain. While there, the three disciples saw Jesus' glory, which was veiled during His earthly ministry with this exception, and they heard a voice from heaven, the Father's, "This is My beloved Son, with whom I am well-pleased; listen to Him" (Matthew 17:5).

To better understand Jesus as a servant it might be helpful if we understood a few details concerning His nature. He is God. He claimed to be God and accepted worship as God (John 20:28) and did things only God can do. Colossians 1:16, 17 states that He created all things and holds all creation in place by the word of His mouth. He stilled an angry sea and told the wind to be still and it instantly obeyed (Mark 4:39)!

As part of the eternal plan of the Triune God, Jesus was incarnated as a human just over 2,000 years ago. Though eternal, His humanity is rather recent (at least compared to His divine nature, which is eternal). His birth was unusual in that He had no earthly, human father, thus avoiding the sin nature all other humans inherit from their fathers (Roman 5:12). Though without a human father, He was fully human, as seen in the traits of humanity he demonstrated. He developed socially, mentally, physically and spiritually (Luke 2:52). As an adult, he demonstrated human traits such as hunger, thirst, and he slept. He was and is God, and since His conception in Mary's womb has been and evermore will be human. He is fully God and fully man. A great description of Him would be, "He is undiminished deity and perfect humanity in one person, the God-man Jesus Christ". Imagine the God-man becoming a servant! Hard to wrap your mind around, isn't it?

Mark's gospel presents Jesus as a servant. Unlike Matthew's gospel which presents Him as a king and proves His claims to David's throne through an extensive genealogy, Mark states He was a servant. Since no one cared about a servant's pedigree - Him family tree - Mark omits it. It has been observed by many in the past that perhaps the key verse to summarize the theme of Mark is found in 10:45, "For even the Son of Man did not come to be served but to serve, and to give His life a ransom for many". Let those words sink in, "...did not come to be served but to serve...." Clearly the greatest act of service ever performed was when Jesus, the God-man, took the sins of all mankind upon Himself and died, the righteous for the unrighteous. Paul's letter to the Christians in Rome says it well, 6:5-11,

For while we were still helpless, at the right time Christ died for the ungodly. For one will hardly die for a righteous man; though perhaps for the good man someone would dare even to die. But God demonstrates His own love toward us, in that while we were yet sinners, Christ died for us. Much more then, having now been justified by His blood, we shall be saved from the wrath *of God* through Him. For if while we were enemies we were reconciled to God through the death of His Son, much more, having been reconciled, we shall be saved by His life. And not only this, but we also exult in God

30

through our Lord Jesus Christ, through whom we have now received the reconciliation.

Notice how we are described by God *before* our salvation - "helpless", "ungodly", "sinners" and "enemies". Now notice how a person is described *after* salvation, which is due primarily to Jesus' service - "justified", "saved" and "reconciled". We've been declared righteous, delivered from sin's eternal consequences (hell and separation from God) and have come to a position of peace! What great truths and the reality for all who believe Jesus' offer for eternal life (John 3:16; 5:24; 6:47; 7:38; 11:25, 26).

Clearly the cross is the greatest demonstration of God's love for us (Romans 5:8) and the ultimate act of service Jesus performed. Yet it is not the only act of service He performed. I am reminded of another time that occurred the evening before the Savior's arrest and crucifixion. The incident is found in John's gospel, chapter 13.

As with every passage of scripture, the context of John 13 is very important. It occurred in an upstairs room in a private residence in Jerusalem. It was the week of Passover and the day was Thursday. The twelve disciples of Jesus had traveled by foot and were about to share a meal together. In middle eastern culture, upon arrival at a private residence, it was customary for the host to direct a servant to wash the feet of the invited guests, since they would be dirty from walking the dirt roads and paths. If the host family was not wealthy enough to have a servant, the member of the family who was considered the "low man on the totem pole" would have been expected to perform the task. It was clearly not a glamorous task. If the cable television show "Dirty Jobs", had existed in that day, it would probably have had an episode devoted to foot washing. Imagine twelve pairs of dirty feet belonging to men who would never have had a pedicure and had generally never taken care of their feet. Given the disciples' mindset that each of them was the greatest of the group, it is no wonder that none of them volunteered to complete the humble task.

Now we enter the heart of the story: "Now before the Feast of the Passover, Jesus knowing that His hour had come that He should depart out of this world to the Father, having loved His own who were in the world, He loved them to the end" (John 13:1). Two truths stand out about Jesus and the timing of this incident; Jesus knew His time on earth was short, yet He was still thinking and acting like a servant. Additionally, in loving the twelve to the end, His love included loving acts of service. Perhaps one of the clearest way to demonstrate you love to others and God is to serve them. Yes, you can tell them, give gifts, take them to special places, and more, but serving demonstrates love as little else does.

The apostle John wrote a few verses later about Jesus' actions, that He "rose from supper, and laid aside His garments; and taking a towel, He girded Himself about. Then He poured water into a basin, and began to wash the disciples' feet, and wipe them with the towel with which He was girded" (John 13:4, 5). Note carefully what Jesus did NOT do, He did not call out in a loud voice, "GENTLEMEN! I am about to model what it means to be a servant". He did not call a press conference to announce the good thing He was about to do. He just performed the task.

Unannounced, Jesus quietly took off His outer garment and wrapped a towel around His waist with which to dry the feet He was about to wash. How unlike the Pharisees that Jesus spoke of in Matthew 6:1-7 - they did good things such as fasting, benevolent giving, and praying, but their motivation was to be seen by others. Essentially, their motivation was the applause of others. There is nothing wrong with people noticing and applauding our works, provided that is not our motivation. One of my mentors used to say, "If you want to know whether you have a servant's heart or not, see how you react when you serve and no one notices". Is your motivation to serve or be noticed? I know there have been plenty of occasions when I did some act that some would have called "service" but when it was not noticed I was disappointed. In those cases, it probably wasn't service, only activity motivated by getting attention. There's an anonymous quote hanging in my office which reads, "It doesn't matter if the world knows, or sees or understands, the only applause we are meant to seek is that of nail-scarred hands".

Years ago, I was a young pastor launching a newly-formed church. We began with about 25 people. So few were we and so tight were the resources that everyone who was a part of our group had many tasks to do. One Friday I was getting our rented facility ready for weekend services and was bent over a toilet, cleaning the bowl. I remember being a bit angry at God and thinking, "I bet NONE of my seminary friends have to clean toilets!" I had a rotten attitude and resented having to do the task. As He is prone to do, the Spirit of God quickly sprang into action and it was almost as if He said, "Your Savior, Jesus, washed feet and took your sins upon Himself as He died on a cross". If the Savior was willing to wash dirty feet, shouldn't we willing to do any task He asks of us? Remember His words, "you also should do as I did to you".

History books tell us that in the ancient Roman empire, the empire of Jesus' day and the New Testament era, approximately 50% of the entire populace were slaves. Slaves were despised and the work they performed was considered menial. Those who had the resources to own servants nearly always did so. Into that sort of culture Jesus was born and during His three to four-year public ministry often served others. Mark's gospel presents Him as a servant. Paul, in Philippians 2:1-11, declares the same truth - that Jesus' humbly served, all the way to a horrible death on a cross.

When we think of God's servants, the first one to come to mind should be Jesus. When followers of Christ speak and think of what it means to become more like our Savior, many traits might come to mind, such as compassion, holiness, truthfulness, and patience. One trait that may not come to mind, but should be near the top of the list, is service. Jesus was God's premier servant.

FOR FURTHER CONSIDERATION

1. Wouldn't it be tragic to be described by
God as a deaf, blind, mute, and disobedient servant?

2. Can you recall a time when you "served" only to
be seen by others?

3. Can you recall a time when you refused to serve
due to the attitude that the act was "beneath" you or
might embarrass you?

4. What act of service is God calling you to
perform that you are hesitating to obey?

CHAPTER 3

MY SERVANT, ABRAHAM

Serving God through Testing

On January 15, 2009, U.S. Airways flight #1549 left New York's LaGuardia Airport bound for Charlotte, North Carolina and then on to the west coast. Within two minutes of takeoff the plane struck several birds which resulted in engine failure. Captain Chesley B. "Sully" Sullenberger safely ditched the plane into the Hudson River. There were 150 people on board and no fatalities!

Was Sully just lucky? Perhaps there might have been some luck involved but a more probable cause is that Sully Sullenberger had logged 19,663 flight hours in his long career (at three hours per flight that would equate to more than 6,500 flights). His flight skills were honed during those boring, nothing's happening sort of days. His long-developed skills prepared him for a defining moment in his life and the lives of 149 other people flying with him that day.

It has been observed, "Character may be manifested in great moments, but it is made in minor events of life". This is especially so in the case of God's servant Abraham whose life is primarily recorded in the book of Genesis. The narrative of his life is told from Genesis chapter 12 through 25. God used decades of experiences and trials to mature Abraham's faith, then one specific day Abraham's character was best demonstrated in his obedient service to God.

Abraham's life began in a place the Bible calls Ur, or more specifically, Ur of the Chaldeans (Genesis 11:24). He lived in a pagan culture and his own family was an idolatrous one. Not a great foundation for being one of the most remarkable people in all the Bible, is it?

When Abram (his birth name which means "exalted father") was 75 years old God, the Creator of the world, the God of the Bible, appeared to him and made some fantastic promises to him. Those promises were unconditional and eternal in nature as well as foundational to much of the rest of scripture. Some of those promises were very personal in nature, "to make Abraham's name great," while others were meant to apply to all people, "through you (Abraham) all the peoples of the earth will be blessed." The apostle Paul understood this promise was fulfilled in Jesus Christ, a descendent of Abraham (Galatians 3:8). Additionally, it was Abraham's descendants, the nation of Israel, who recorded and largely preserved the Bible.

About the same time God appeared to Abram to give him these promises, God changed his name to Abraham which means, "father of a multitude". The irony of Abram's birth name, "exalted father" and his God-given name, "father of a multitude" must have been a bit of a pill for Abraham to swallow as he had no children.

At some point, which the scriptures do not pinpoint for us, Abraham believed God's promise to provide a Deliverer and God declared him to be righteous, He justified him (Genesis 15:6).

Abraham and Sarah knew God's promise of a son, but after a decade of waiting their faith faltered and they resorted to a culturally accepted practice to "help" God fulfill His promise. The culturally accepted practice, though a heinous sin in God's sight, was to give a female servant, Hagar, to Abraham to father a child by her. The child would be considered Abraham and Sarah's, because Hagar was their "property". How that act must have displeased God! Abraham and Sarah were unbelieving that God could fulfill His promise. God has never needed assistance in fulfilling His promises; He who created the world with His word can easily do what He says, including having an old childless couple conceive and happily await the birth of their first child - the child of promise.

Finally, at age 100 Abraham became a father to Isaac, whose name means "laughter". His name's meaning was a daily reminder that when his impending conception and birth was announced by the angel of the Lord, Sarah had laughed in unbelief. So too it was a reminder that God had brought laughter to this older couple's home.

Be assured that God's timing is rarely our timing. Isaac was born much later than Abraham and Sarah wanted and thought he should have been. Know also that God can turn sorrow into joy and laughter as He did with Abraham. He'll do that one day for every believer as He raptures us to heaven and gives us each a glorified body, no longer subject to sickness and sinful practices, and unites us with those who also believed Him yet have preceded us in death.

Abraham's great compliment

Years later when Isaac was a man, God spoke to him: "the Lord appeared to him the same night and said, 'I am the God of your father Abraham; do not fear, for I am with you. I will bless you and multiply your descendants for the sake of *My servant Abraham*'" (emphasis mine;

Genesis 26:24). When God spoke to Isaac and referred to his father He used the phrase, "My servant Abraham". What a powerful statement! Imagine God describing you to your children or your friends or co-workers. Are you living in such a manner that God would describe you that way? Many live so that others would describe them as "successful" or "prominent". There have been many times when I've wished others would describe me as a great athlete, great preacher, the best father, and more, but how much greater would it be if God were to praise us? It was high praise for God to describe Abraham as His servant.

Stephen Covey in his 1980's best seller, *7 Habits of Highly Effective People,* challenges his readers to consider their own funerals; who do they envision will be present? What do they hope others would say about them? Covey then challenges the reader to live life in such a way that what they hope people would say, would actually be said if a funeral were to take place. To put it bluntly, if you want God to describe you as "My servant" you must serve and obey Him.

Previously we referenced Sully Sullenberger's biggest test as a pilot. What about Abraham's biggest test? It is recorded in Genesis chapter 22. In the first three verses, we read:

"Now it came about after these things, that God tested Abraham, and said to him, 'Abraham' and he said, 'Here I am'. And He said, 'Take now your only son whom you love, Isaac, and go to the land of Moriah; and offer him there as a burnt offering on one of the mountains of which I will tell you'. So Abraham rose early in the morning and saddled his donkey, and took two of his young men with him and Isaac his son; and he split wood for the burnt offering, and rose and went to the place of which God had told him."

The severity of the test could hardly be overestimated. God was asking, no commanding Abraham to offer up his one and only dearly loved son. In the response of Abraham, three truths emerge:

1. *Abraham Immediately Obeyed His Master*

Notice the words, "...so Abraham rose early in the morning and saddled his donkey". Abraham did not say to the Lord, "Lord let me pray about this matter" (that's often a "Christian" way of saying "no"). He did not delay. Apparently, God spoke to him in the evening or perhaps while He was sleeping, during a dream. Apparently, Abraham obeyed the next morning as soon as it was light enough to travel. Note also that Abraham did not rationalize, "but Lord, he's my only son!" He didn't procrastinate by telling the Lord, "Let me have him for one more month, then I'll obey your voice. I am confident the reason for this immediate obedience was due to this fact: Abraham understood he had a Master, not an advisor. Advisors give advice and we can take it or leave it. Masters give orders and servants are expected to obey them.

For more than 25 years I have lived with a few miles of the United States Army's largest base, Fort Bragg. It currently is home to nearly 60,000 active duty soldiers. While I have never personally been in the military, I have come to appreciate many things about soldiers. One is their understanding of and commitment to obeying authority.

We would do well to imitate Abraham's instant obedience. Our Master has given us many commands - they include:

- To forgive others, as God in Christ, has forgiven us (Ephesians 4:32).
- To share the good news of Christ's offer of forgiveness and life. In one major denomination in the U.S., 90% reported they'd NEVER obeyed this command once!
- To give generously of material resources God has entrusted to us as His managers.
- To use the spiritual gift(s) we've been given for the glory of the Giver and the good of the church, which is the body of Christ.

When we read or hear scripture proclaimed one question we should ask is, "is there a command for me to obey"? If yes, do it.

2. Abraham was convinced his Master would provide.

As Abraham, Isaac, and two unnamed servants headed off to the God-appointed place of sacrifice, a conversation ensued. Genesis 22:4-8 records the conversation for us:

> On the third day Abraham raised his eyes and saw the place from a distance. Abraham said to his young men, "Stay here with the donkey, and I and the lad will go over there; and we will worship and return to you." Abraham took the wood of the burnt offering and laid it on Isaac his son, and he took in his hand the fire and the knife. So the two of them walked on together. Isaac spoke to Abraham his father and said, "My father!" And he said, "Here I am, my son." And he said, "Behold, the fire and the wood, but where is the lamb for the burnt offering?" Abraham said, "God will provide for Himself the lamb for the burnt offering, my son." So the two of them walked on together.

Isaac, apparently a young man by now since he was able to carry all the wood necessary for the sacrifice, made an important observation and asked an astute question. The observation? "Dad, we have the wood, we've got a torch for fire, we've got all we need except…". The question, "Dad, where's the sacrificial animal? I don't see a lamb, a goat, or any other suitable animal."

Abraham's response is classic. He told Isaac, "God will provide." Literally, he said, "God will see to it." In modern vernacular, "God will take care of it, son." If God wants a sacrifice, He'll see to it that one is provided. Abraham uses, for the first time in scripture, the name of God, "Jehovah-Jireh" which means "God will provide".

Consider for a moment a few times God, Jehovah-Jireh, has provided for His people:

- Six times weekly for nearly forty years, He rained bread from heaven to feed nearly three million people in the wilderness.
- In Babylon, He provided protection for Shadrach, Meshach and Ebed-nego in a fiery furnace and for their friend Daniel in a lion's den.
- Greatest of all, He provided a Savior for what seemed to be a hopeless group of rebels!

Events like these proclaim the greatness of the God who performed them. What a provider we have! Abraham simply believed Jehovah-Jireh would live up to His name.

At the human level, this passage also teaches us about faith. Faith is simply believing something to be true based upon the evidence one has been given. After 50+ years of walking with God, Abraham had been given ample evidence that his God was Jehovah-Jireh, the provider. Because of his faith, Abraham acted in obedience by going to the appointed place of sacrifice and he expected God would do something, though he didn't know what that would be.

I enjoy playing games that require knowledge rather than luck (roll of the dice). One game I play on occasion has six categories of trivia questions. I am confident in three of the categories and increasingly less confident in the other three with the entertainment category being my worst. Often, I merely guess from the multiple-choice answers I am given. Unlike my knowledge of the entertainment category, Abraham had a mature knowledge of God and thus a confidence in God's provision.

God has given a command to you to be generous and He will supply all your needs (Philippians 4:19). Are you confident in His ability and faithfulness? So confident that you obey?

Our Provider has also commanded us to share the good news of Christ's death, burial, and resurrection and His offer of forgiveness and life to all who will believe His promise. He's promised to assist us in evangelism and convict those who hear the truth. Do you act on those commands and promises from the Provider?

3. *Abraham was convinced of His Master's ability to do the impossible.*

The scene that unfolded next is one of the most poignant in the entire Bible. Here's what happened, it found in Genesis 22:9-14:

Then they came to the place of which God had told him; and Abraham built the altar there and arranged the wood, and bound his son Isaac and laid him on the altar, on top of the wood. Abraham stretched out his hand and took the knife to slay his son. But the angel of the LORD called to him from heaven and said, "Abraham, Abraham!" And he said, "Here I am." He said, "Do not stretch out your hand against the lad, and do nothing to him; for now, I know that you fear God, since you have not withheld your son, your only son, from Me." Then Abraham raised his eyes and looked, and behold, behind *him* a ram caught in the thicket by his horns; and Abraham went and took the ram and offered him up for a burnt offering in the place of his son. Abraham called the name of that place The LORD Will Provide, as it is said to this day, "In the mount of the LORD it will be provided."

You'll notice that in Abraham's faith he told his two servants that he and Isaac would go and ***return.*** Again, Abraham did not know how this would happen - only that it could and would. After traveling a distance, father and son came to the God-appointed place. Isaac allowed himself to be bound and placed upon the sacrificial altar. Abraham raised the knife in his hand to obey God's command. If this were a movie, we'd be tempted to hit the "pause" button. If we were viewing the scene live, we'd want to yell, "Abraham, stop! What are you doing?!" Often when we read our Bibles, we'd like to know more details about the story than what are given, but normally we are not privy to such knowledge. In this case the New Testament informs the reader of what Abraham was thinking. In Hebrews chapter 11, that great "Hall of Fame of Faith" chapter, the writer of Hebrews brags about Abraham. He tells us what Abraham was thinking at this moment. Hebrews 11:17-19 says,

> By faith Abraham, when he was tested, offered up Isaac, and he who had received the promises was offering up his only begotten *son*; *it was he* to whom it was said, "IN ISAAC YOUR DESCENDANTS SHALL BE CALLED." He considered that God is able to raise *people* even from the dead, from which he also received him back as a type.

Abraham's understanding of God was that if God wanted him to take his son's life, God was able and would restore Isaac because God had already told him this was the son of promise; and descendants as innumerable as the stars of the sky or as the grains of sand on the beach must come from him. Isaac can't father children while dead! Therefore, Abraham concluded God was able "to raise back to life" (11:19)! Remember this was more than 1,000 years before God used Elijah to raise the widow's son to life. It was twenty centuries before Jesus raised Lazarus to life after he was dead for four days. It was also twenty centuries before the first Easter. Abraham believed not only

53

that God was powerful but also faithful to fulfill His promises.

What about you? Has God made any promises that at this moment seem impossible, or least highly unlikely, to come to fruition? How about avenging a wrong if you choose to forgive someone else? How about meeting your needs if you give sacrificially to Christ-centered ministries? Does the abundant life, a life to the fullest, seem impossible?

Are you like me - at times over-promising and under-delivering? Not that we do it intentionally, but sometimes our mouths get us in trouble. God NEVER makes promises that He cannot later fulfill. Neither does He make promises that He has no intention of fulfilling. Abraham believed his Master could and would do what seemed impossible (raise a dead son to life) though a resurrection had never occurred in human history.

In His twilight years, Abraham faced his biggest test. The test came from God but was not given until God had prepared him in the smaller tests of life. Could it be that God has brought you to the threshold of your biggest test to date? I don't know what it might be, but know this from Abraham's life, it could well be the greatest opportunity of your life to serve God. Hundreds of millions of people have read and been encouraged by this event since it first occurred nearly 4,000 years ago.

When facing our trials/tests, God's servant Abraham teaches us three things:

- Serve God immediately; He's a Master, not an advisor.
- Trust God to provide whatever He requires of you.
- Trust God to be faithful to do what He promised, even if it seems impossible.

FOR FURTHER CONSIDERATION:

1. If God were to describe you to your children, spouse, or others, what descriptive trait do you think He would use?

2. Looking back on life, can you see how God grew your faith in smaller tests to prepare you for bigger ones?

3. So far on your life's journey, what has been your biggest test of faith?

4. Can you recall a time when God did the "impossible" for you? What was it?

Chapter Four

My Servant, Moses

Serving God during opposition

If you're around people for any length of time, you will experience opposition from some folks. It might be mild but could be quite severe. Domestic disputes are calls law enforcement officers dread and ones that often turn violent. If you have siblings, you know a bit about sibling rivalry. Yes, family can be the source of great opposition. Those who know us well are often the first to oppose. Jesus himself said that a prophet was not without honor except in his own hometown. The gospel of Mark tells us, "And when His own people (eg. kinsmen/family) heard of this, they went out to take custody of Him; for they were saying, 'He has lost His senses'" (3:21). Jesus' half-brothers and sisters thought He was a bit "off". In modern vernacular, they wanted to have Him "committed".

Opposition doesn't only come from family, it can come from other places too. Ask any pastor, he'll tell you his greatest opposition has come from those within the church membership. Most employees will tell you the greatest troubles they face at work don't come from customers but from fellow employees. Whether from family members, co-workers, neighbors, or friends, everyone at some time or another will experience opposition. When, not if, we face opposition - how should we respond? How do we respond?

Moses faced opposition at many points of his life - from the pharaoh of Egypt, from the people of Israel in the wilderness, and from his own siblings. More is written about Moses than any other person in the Bible except for Jesus Christ. He was born in Egypt soon after an edict from the pharaoh declared all baby boys born to Jewish parents were to be murdered as a means of population control. Fortunately, Moses' parents disobeyed the command and his life was spared. He was "adopted" by pharaoh's daughter after she found him in a basket in the Nile River. He spent the first forty years of his life in a palace in Egypt, with all the riches, education, and pleasures such a place had to offer. All the while his kinsmen, Abraham's descendants, suffered as slaves for Egypt's economy and great building projects.

At age 40 he became a fugitive after he murdered an Egyptian who was abusing a Jewish slave. When his deed became known, he was forced to flee for his life. He lived as a shepherd in Midian until God suddenly and miraculously appeared to him to call and commission him as His prophet and the vehicle He would use to cause Israel's deliverance. It was only one or two years after God used the ten plagues to free Israel from oppression and they were on their journey toward God's promised land that Moses faced his sternest opposition.

The story of Moses' opposition is recorded in Numbers chapter 12. It occurred at least 14 months after the exodus (see Numbers 10:11) and soon after the serious complaint by the nation of Israel over the lack of meat in their diet (Numbers 11).

Numbers 12:1-3 opens with the following:

Then Miriam and Aaron spoke against Moses because of the Cushite woman whom he had married (for he had married a Cushite woman); and they said, "Has the LORD indeed spoken only through Moses? Has He not spoken through us as well?" And the LORD heard it. (Now the man Moses was very humble, more than any man who was on the face of the earth.)

Apparently, Moses' siblings Miriam and Aaron objected to Moses' marriage. They also objected to his leadership and used the occasion to voice their strong opinion, "You're not the only one God speaks to/through!" In modern terms they declared, "Who died and put you in charge?!" One can imagine their jealousy - their little brother was the boss over them!

God defends His servant

Moses didn't say to his siblings, "stop opposing me, remember I am a servant of Jehovah!" It was God who defended him, saying of him, "My servant, Moses...." It must have been wonderfully encouraging for Moses to not only hear that tribute spoken of him but also to consider the circumstances in which they were uttered. God had

defended him before his opposition, Moses didn't
need to defend himself.

God's description of His servant

1. Moses was a humble servant. To be called
"humble", meek in some of the older English Bible
translations, is NOT considered a compliment in
today's culture. In our day a humble person is a
person who looks down at the ground, never
looking at others in the eye. For many today to be
humble means to not have much of a backbone. To
use the term "meek" of a person, especially a man,
in our culture often conjures up pictures of a wimp.
Nothing could be further from the truth. To be
humble, a term used only thirteen times in the Old
Testament, meant "to be gentle, lowly, meek,
humble; self-abased." It does not mean having no
conviction or backbone. Remember this same
humble Moses strode into Pharaoh's presence ten
times to demand, "Let my people go!" It has been
said the of word humble that it was occasionally
used in ancient culture to describe a horse that had

been bridled or "broken" to a bit in its mouth. Before it was humbled, the horse had immense strength. But after the horse was broken, the strength was now a harnessed, controlled, productive strength. Before Moses had become humble, he had strength enough to kill an Egyptian with his bare hands. Now his strength of character and resolve was harnessed and he allowed God to use him powerfully.

When Moses was challenged by his two older siblings, he didn't respond in arrogance - that God had called and spoken to him directly (true). He didn't remind them that while they had been slaves, he had been educated in the finest "university" Egypt had to offer (also true). In humility Moses let God defend him.

It is of interest to me that the term "meek" is used only four times in the entire New Testament. Twice it is used by Jesus to describe himself (Matthew 10:28, 29), yet it was this same Jesus who twice cleansed the temple with whips to drive out money changers and livestock traders. Once the term meek is used of how a wife should behave toward her unsaved husband. Why? So that her "meekness" - her strength that's been harnessed by God's Spirit and a deliberate act of her will - might be the catalyst God uses to bring about her husband's conversion (1 Peter 3:1-4).

When - not if - you are opposed by others, whether at work, on the team, in the neighborhood, or even under your own roof, do you lose control and exert yourself sinfully? Put another way, are your strengths harnessed by the Holy Spirit?

2. Moses was faithful in opposition.

We know that Aaron was three years older than Moses (Exodus 7:7). We also know that Miriam was older than Moses as she was charged with watching him when he was placed in a basket in the Nile as an infant. She also was old enough to have the wisdom to offer to get her mother to nurse Moses after he had been found by Pharaoh's daughter (Exodus 2:4, 7). Perhaps Miriam was 8-10 years older than Moses. Moses was clearly Aaron and Miriam's little brother and it appears they were jealous of him. Numbers 12:4-8 states,

Suddenly the LORD said to Moses and Aaron and to Miriam, "You three come out to the tent of meeting." So the three of them came out. Then the LORD came down in a pillar of cloud and stood at the doorway of the tent, and He called Aaron and Miriam. When they had both come forward, He said, "Hear now My words: If there is a prophet among you, I, the LORD, shall make Myself known to him in a vision. I shall speak with him in a dream. "Not so, with My servant Moses, He is faithful in all My household; With him I speak mouth to mouth, even openly, and not in dark sayings, and he beholds the form of the LORD. Why then were you not afraid To speak against My servant, against Moses?"

God called the three siblings to come to meet Him. Can you imagine how scared Miriam and Aaron must have been when God said, "You three, front and center!" When I was a young boy if you got in trouble in school the teacher would say, "go to the principal's office!" It only happened to me once, but I still remember it like it was yesterday. In those days principals did not hesitate to apply the "board of education" to the "seat" of knowledge, if you catch my drift. As scared as I was to be in Mr. Kubic's office, can you imagine Miriam and Aaron's fear as they stood before God?

God describes His servant, their little brother, using the term "faithful". The Hebrew word means, "true, trusty, verified; to be firm; permanent." To be firm is the opposite of wobbly or unstable. Something that has not been verified is not trusted. Ever had an older vehicle that began to act up? One time you couldn't get it started, a few weeks later it overheated. Finally, one day while running errands it died in the parking lot. After a few such incidents like those, you would have lost all confidence in the vehicle because it is NOT faithful or trustworthy.

Paul, in his first letter to the church at Corinth, wrote, "In this case, moreover, it is required of stewards that one be found trustworthy" (4:2). As an overarching quality, God is looking for faithfulness in His people. He is NOT looking for perfection, great intelligence, power, or beauty. He will evaluate His children based on their faithfulness.

George MacDonald, a 19th century Scottish pastor and writer whose books were greatly influential in bringing C. S. Lewis to faith, once wrote, "It is a greater compliment to be trusted than to be loved". Ponder that - you might choose to love anyone, even the "unlovely," but you only trust those who are faithful and trustworthy.

Do others trust you? When you give your word, do you keep it? When you volunteer, can others rely on your word, or do they need a signed contract? If God were to offer an oral or written evaluation of your life, would He say or write, "Faithful"?

3. Moses was a compassionate servant.
Remember that, Aaron and Miriam had challenged Moses' leadership. They claimed that he was not the only one God spoke to – that they were spokespersons of God too. As a man with siblings, who also shared a few sibling rivalry moments, I might have been tempted to say, "Lord discipline them, they started this fight!" Or when God disciplined them, "Na-na-na-na-na!" In my younger days, when dad or mom wasn't looking, I'd have

stuck out my tongue at them. Unlike me, Moses'
response was much godlier. Numbers 12:9-13:

> So the anger of the LORD burned against them and He
> departed. But when the cloud had withdrawn from over the
> tent, behold, Miriam *was* leprous, as *white as* snow. As Aaron
> turned toward Miriam, behold, she *was* leprous. Then Aaron
> said to Moses, "Oh, my lord, I beg you, do not account *this* sin
> to us, in which we have acted foolishly and in which we have
> sinned. Oh, do not let her be like one dead, whose flesh is half
> eaten away when he comes from his mother's womb!" Moses
> cried out to the LORD, saying, "O God, heal her, I pray!"

As an act of discipline, God struck Miriam with
leprosy. Probably she had instigated the incident, so
Aaron was spared. The compassion Moses
demonstrated was taken to another level when
another Servant, Jesus Christ, said from the cross,
"Father forgive them for they know not what they
do" (Luke 23:34).

When your spouse, your kids, your co-workers
think of you, do they think, "she's such a
compassionate person?" Or do they think, "he's
quite a vengeful person, holds a grudge, and, like a
pit-bull, refuses to let go of a wrong suffered"?

Moses, a choice servant of the Father,
demonstrated a great depth of character in a severe
time of opposition. When some of the people

closest to him attacked, he demonstrated a depth of character. He was faithful, humble, and compassionate. May those same qualities be true of us too.

Moses' life teaches us many things, but the incident in Numbers 12 lets us know that perhaps our greatest opportunity to serve God and glorify His name will be during a time of opposition from those who are closest to us.

FOR FURTHER CONSIDERATION:

1. Are you living in such a manner that if you were opposed by others and God were to defend you, He would say, "that's My servant!"?

2. How can strengths and humility/meekness go hand in hand?

3. If your life is not currently characterized by faithfulness, what can you do so that will be a character trait that you ARE known for?

4. Can you recall a time when you were in the wrong and another believer exhibited great compassion to you? How did that make you feel?

Chapter Five

My servant, Caleb

Serving God in the Minority

We don't like being in the minority in any area of our lives. Do you recall being in a setting where you were the only person wearing a certain style of shoe while everyone else was wearing something different and more fashionable? How about being the only gentleman in an upscale restaurant who did not have on a coat and tie? I grew up in the Midwest, in Oklahoma to be exact. I'm a huge Sooner fan. I don't like being in a room full of Longhorns, Huskers, or Cowboys when I'm the only Sooner in the room (especially when the crimson and cream are losing). Ever voted and your candidate lost in a landslide, not even close?

Yes, we hate being in the minority. It's far easier to live life when you're surrounded by people who hold to the same convictions and beliefs you do. Imagine being in a group where you are in the minority - only 16% hold to your view on a certain topic. What would it be like to be in the minority of 2 out of as many as 3,000,000 people?

How should we live, what character should God's servant display when in the minority? One of God's servants gives us aspiring servants a great example. His story is found in the book of Numbers, chapter 14.

Before we consider his story, a bit of background information might be helpful. After four long centuries (400 years) God had powerfully and miraculously delivered the nation of Israel using Moses as the human deliverer. God's great power was on full display when He parted the Red Sea for Israel and closed it on the Egyptian army. Israel was now journeying to the land God had promised and Moses sent twelve leaders, one from each of the tribes of Israel to spy out the land (Numbers 13:2). Each of the men was a leader, in fact the scriptures say each was "distinguished". The twelve were given a task - spy out the land and bring back a report on the people and the conditions of the land.

The names of the twelve spies are listed in Numbers 13. Chances are good you would not recognize the names of 10 of the 12…they are somewhat forgotten or ignored. The two names you'd probably recognize? Joshua and Caleb. In biblical times, names were often chosen with care as to their meaning. We choose names based upon the sound or because it's a family name or a trendy name. Elijah means "My God is Jehovah" Abraham means "father of a multitude", Joshua means "God saves" or "salvation is of Jehovah." Daniel means "God is my judge." Zechariah means "God remembers." You get the point. You might ask, what does Caleb's name mean? In light of the previous list, you might want to sit down… oh wait, you're reading so most likely you are sitting down. Caleb's name means "dog". In that culture, typically the father of the child chose the name. Caleb's father was Jephunneh. If we were to ask Jephunneh, "why did you name your son 'dog'", I suspect he might say, "we were treated like dogs when we labored in slavery in Egypt". Caleb spent the first forty years of his life as a member of a nation of slaves, treated like dogs by their oppressors.

Other than having a name that had a bit of an unusual meaning, being a slave in Egypt early in life, and being a leader of his tribe and therefore chosen to be one of twelve to spy out the land of promise, what do we know about this servant of God? What did his Master say about him?

In Numbers 14:24, God said the following, "But My Servant Caleb, because he has had a different spirit and has followed Me fully, I will bring into the land which he entered, and his descendants shall take possession of it." God made two descriptive statements about His servant and one promise about him.

Caleb had a different spirit

You'll notice in our English translations of the Bible, the word "spirit" is not capitalized. In the original Hebrew the word for the Spirit of God, the Holy Spirit, and the word for a person's spirit, the non-physical part of a person, are the same word. It is the context that determines which concept is being referred to. Here the context is clearly referring to Caleb's personality, not the Spirit of God. God is not saying Caleb is odd, as when we say, "my neighbor is different." He is saying Caleb is unique, he's different from the majority.

Do you remember what the majority, the ten spies who didn't agree with Caleb and Joshua's report had said? Let's remind ourselves:

When they returned from spying out the land, at the end of forty days, they proceeded to come to Moses and Aaron and to all the congregation of the sons of Israel in the wilderness of Paran, at Kadesh; and they brought back word to them and to all the congregation and showed them the fruit of the land. Thus they told him, and said, "We went in to the land where you sent us; and it certainly does flow with milk and honey, and this is its fruit. Nevertheless, the people who live in the land are strong, and the cities are fortified *and* very large; and moreover, we saw the descendants of Anak there. Amalek is living in the land of the Negev and the Hittites and the Jebusites and the Amorites are living in the hill country, and the Canaanites are living by the sea and by the side of the Jordan."
But the men who had gone up with him said, "We are not able to go up against the people, for they are too strong for us." So they gave out to the sons of Israel a bad report of the land which they had spied out, saying, "The land through which we have gone, in spying it out, is a land that devours

its inhabitants; and all the people whom we saw in it are men of *great* size. There also we saw the Nephilim (the sons of Anak are part of the Nephilim); and we became like grasshoppers in our own sight, and so we were in their sight." Numbers 13:25-29, 31-33

Essentially, they reported to Moses and all of Israel, "indeed the land is abundant, its natural resources are many, the crops are productive, it's just as God told us, BUT the people there are physically imposing and if we were to enter into a battle with them, they'd easily defeat us".

You might be tempted to say, "well that was only those ten leaders, most of Israel didn't feel that way, did they?" Again, we would do well to see what God's report of the multitude was. It's found in Numbers 14:1-4, 22, 23:

Then all the congregation lifted up their voices and cried, and the people wept that night. All the sons of Israel grumbled against Moses and Aaron; and the whole congregation said to them, "Would that we had died in the land of Egypt! Or would that we had died in this wilderness! Why is the LORD bringing us into this land, to fall by the sword? Our wives and our little ones will become plunder; would it not be better for us to return to Egypt?" So they said to one another, "Let us appoint a leader and return to Egypt."
Surely all the men who have seen My glory and My signs which I performed in Egypt and in the wilderness, yet have put Me to the test these ten times and have not listened to My voice, shall by no means see the land which I swore to their fathers, nor shall any of those who spurned Me see it.

78

The multitude, who were influenced by the ten, concluded, "We'll die. Our wives and children will be spoils to be raped, enslaved, or murdered. Slavery is a certain future if we engage in battle. Our biggest problem is we need a new leader!" College and professional sports fans often respond the same way on that last point. We need a new coach if we want to get to where we want to go. So, ten of the twelve spies and the entire multitude of adults believed the majority opinion and voiced their sentiment.

In contrast to that sort of sentiment we read about Caleb's different spirit. It was different in that it was rare, not common. Remember He had seen precisely the same sights as the ten spies who offered a discouraging report. Look at what he said to the multitude. Numbers 14:6-9 states:

Joshua the son of Nun and Caleb the son of Jephunneh, of those who had spied out the land, tore their clothes; and they spoke to all the congregation of the sons of Israel, saying, "The land which we passed through to spy out is an exceedingly good land. If the LORD is pleased with us, then He will bring us into this land and give it to us—a land which flows with milk and honey. Only do not rebel against the LORD; and do not fear the people of the land, for they will be our prey. Their protection has been removed from them, and the LORD is with us; do not fear them."

Caleb was convinced the land already belonged to Israel. He encouraged his countrymen to not fear. He saw the people, though big, as unprotected! How could he conclude this? Because, as he said, "God is with us."

Still, one is left to wonder why he drew such a vastly different conclusion from the majority. I am convinced it was due to the promises of God given to Abraham many years before in Genesis 15:13-21. It includes some very great promises to Abraham and his descendants, of whom Caleb was:

God said to Abram, "Know for certain that your descendants will be strangers in a land that is not theirs, where they will be enslaved and oppressed four hundred years. But I will also judge the nation whom they will serve, and afterward they will come out with many possessions. As for you, you shall go to your fathers in peace; you will be buried at a good old age. Then in the fourth generation they will return here, for the iniquity of the Amorite is not yet complete." It came about when the sun had set, that it was very dark, and behold, *there appeared* a smoking oven and a flaming torch which passed between these pieces. On that day the LORD made a covenant with Abram, saying, "To your descendants I have given this land, from the river of Egypt as far as the great river, the river Euphrates: the Kenite and the Kenizzite and the Kadmonite and the Hittite and the Perizzite and the Rephaim and the Amorite and the Canaanite and the Girgashite and the Jebusite."

Essentially, Caleb believed God would be faithful to His promise and thus he believed in God's protection.

All this leads me to ask a few questions. Am I different from the crowds, the majority - even different from most others who name the name of Christ? Are you? When the stock market takes a dive and adversely affects your retirement nest egg, are you different than others in your response? When the election doesn't yield the results you'd hoped for? When the doctor's report isn't the news you'd hoped to receive? How about in your management of finances…is generosity toward Christ-centered ministries high on your agenda?

It seems to me that believers in Christ only have two options. We either have big problems and a small God OR we have a big God and small problems.

Like Caleb of old you too will have a different spirit when you let the Spirit of God, who indwells

all believers, consistently control you (Ephesians
5:18-21).

Caleb followed God fully

What does it mean to follow God fully? It
might be helpful to determine what it does not mean
first. It does not mean to follow God *perfectly*.
Here it seems to carry the idea of following God
unreservedly or *completely*. Caleb did not attempt
to compartmentalize his life and then offer God a
portion of it (e.g., "God, I'll give you my
relationships and finances.)

In the New Testament, fourteen centuries after
Caleb's story, the apostle Paul penned these words:

Therefore I urge you, brethren, by the mercies of God,
to present your bodies a living and holy sacrifice, acceptable
to God, *which is* your spiritual service of worship. And do
not be conformed to this world, but be transformed by
the renewing of your mind, so that you may prove what the
will of God is, that which is good and acceptable and perfect,
Romans 12:1, 2.

We're not commanded to give the Lord certain parts
of our bodies (e.g. heart, mind, or eyes) but all of
ourselves. It's the only reasonable response we

could offer considering God's great mercies to us, His children.

Robert Munger in his classic booklet, *My Heart, Christ's Home,* pictures our lives like homes and Jesus like a guest who knocks at the door and invites Himself in. He is not content to be just a guest, only allowed into the living room. He would like access to every room and closet in the house. Have you ever completely dedicated your entire self to Jesus? In one sense, that's a picture of who Caleb was - an unreserved servant of the Lord. Perhaps you've heard a powerful sermon or a been to life-altering weekend retreat and made a commitment to follow Jesus wholeheartedly. The unfortunate truth is that many a person has done this only to wander from the commitment months or a few years later. I find it quite interesting that this was NOT the case with Caleb. The story in Numbers occurred when Caleb was in his early forties. When we look at his life in the book of Joshua, 40 years have passed since he returned from spying out the land - forty years since God's declaration and praise of him and his unreserved devotion. Joshua 14:6-15 tells us the following:

Then the sons of Judah drew near to Joshua in Gilgal, and Caleb the son of Jephunneh the Kenizzite said to him, "You know the word which the LORD spoke to Moses the man of God concerning you and me in Kadesh-barnea. I was forty years old when Moses the servant of the LORD sent me from Kadesh-barnea to spy out the land, and I brought word back to him as *it was* in my heart. Nevertheless my brethren who went up with me made the heart of the people melt with fear; but I followed the LORD my God fully. So Moses swore on that day, saying, 'Surely the land on which your foot has trodden will be an inheritance to you and to your children forever, because you have followed the LORD my God fully.' Now behold, the LORD has let me live, just as He spoke, these forty-five years, from the time that the LORD spoke this word to Moses, when Israel walked in the wilderness; and now behold, I am eighty-five years old today. I am still as strong today as I was in the day Moses sent me; as my strength was then, so my strength is now, for war and for going out and coming in. Now then, give me this hill country about which the LORD spoke on that day, for you heard on that day that Anakim *were* there, with great fortified cities; perhaps the LORD will be with me, and I will drive them out as the LORD has spoken." So Joshua blessed him and gave Hebron to Caleb the son of Jephunneh for an inheritance. Therefore, Hebron became the inheritance of Caleb the son of Jephunneh the Kenizzite until this day, because he followed the LORD God of Israel fully. Now the name of Hebron was formerly Kiriath-arba; *for Arba* was the greatest man among the Anakim. Then the land had rest from war.

Notice how it is said by Caleb or of Caleb that he followed God "fully" and it says so three times! It is also remarkable that this occurred when he was

85 years old. At that age, he was ready to take on new challenges, big challenges.

How about you? Have you given up on new challenges as you've aged, or are you regularly tackling new adventures for Jesus? What ministry opportunity are you planning to tackle in the next few months? Is there a long-cherished sin in your life that needs to be addressed frankly and ruthlessly? When comparing your life to a race, are you sprinting toward the finish line or sitting this one out on the recliner?

God's promise to Caleb

Not only does God take note of Caleb by mentioning he had a different spirit and that he had followed Him fully, He also made a promise to Caleb. What did God promise his servant? Numbers 14:24 says, "…*because* he has had a different spirit and has followed Me fully, I will bring into the land which he entered, and his descendants shall take possession of it." All ten spies who doubted God and the rest of that generation would not enter the land. Caleb would enter it, though it took forty-plus years for the promise to be realized. There's a wonderful lesson for us - God's timing is rarely the same as ours. We prefer quick, micro-wave results but God often does His work with a sun-dial, crock pot time frame. Additionally, the promise was that Caleb's descendants would be blessed because of his obedience! His life would result in blessings to the next generation and beyond. In their case, it would be taking possession of a portion of land. On a personal note, my life has been immeasurably blessed because of the faithful service and lives of my parents. They both taught me and my siblings many traits: what it meant to live a godly life, how to be generous with God's resources, what it meant to open one's home to others, and more.

How about you? Are you living in such a way that your children, grandchildren, and others are blessed because of your life?

Do you remember what Caleb's name meant? Caleb means "dog". As I write this I have two dogs. Mollie is an Australian Shepherd, an "Aussie" for short. She's a pure-bred dog that we got as a puppy. She's as smart a dog as I've ever had. We have to spell about 25 different words when she's in the room (like you would when a 3 or 4-year-old child is present) or else she knows what we said. Our other dog is Oscar, a mixed breed male - what was once called a mutt but now is designated an All-American by the American Kennel Club. He was a pet rescue that lived the first 15 months of his life in a shelter with more than 500 other dogs and cats. The shelter was later closed for animal cruelty. When Oscar was born, he had a "club" foot/paw for his front right leg. He is frightened of everything. As you might imagine, with a bad foot, being skittish of everything, and being 15 months old, he was basically unadoptable. One day my youngest daughter and wife saw him at an adoption event with his head down while all the people at the event passed right by looking for a puppy or kitten. They both were drawn to him and within 30 minutes we had another dog. While

Oscar has some issues, he is by far the most loyal dog I have ever owned. He follows me everywhere and sleeps at my feet when I sit in my recliner.

Clearly, I don't know what goes through the mind of a dog but I have a suspicion that Oscar is thankful for being rescued from a miserable, deplorable and hopeless situation. Therefore, he is loyal to the family who gained his freedom. You know there's a bit of Oscar and Caleb, the "dog", in all of us who have believed Jesus' promise for eternal life. We too have been treated like dogs by a former master but then were adopted into a new, eternal family. The "fee" for our adoption was the precious blood of our new Master. Since we have been rescued from such a deplorable situation, we too should loyally serve Him. We are truly special needs "dogs". We may not have any physical issues, but we sure do have many spiritual ones. It is we who should have different spirits and unreservedly, follow God.

Caleb's life is a great example of serving God while in the minority. He did not care that the ten spies said they could not win a battle, nor that the entire nation sided with them. He believed God would keep His promises and thus he had a different spirit and followed God fully.

In the 4th century A.D. a man by the name of Athanasius had a different spirit and followed God fully. He was arrested for following God and put on trial and condemned to death at the stake. When bound to the stake, an official, hoping to cause him to renounce Jesus, said, "Athanasius, don't you know the whole world is against you?!" To which Athanasius responded, "then I am against the whole world!" May his tribe increase. Will you be like Caleb and Athanasius and serve though no one else does?

FOR FURTHER CONSIDERATION

1. Recall a time when you were in the stark minority...how did that make you feel?

2. Do you remember a time when you did something you knew was wrong but you did it because everyone else was too?

3. Why do you think Caleb's response was so different than the majority even though the other spies saw the same things?

4. Have you ever felt you were unreservedly following God? What was that like?

5. If you're not following God full right now, why not? What's holding you back?

Chapter Six

My Servant, Job

Serving God through Suffering

In the fall of 1949 a baby girl was born into a family in Baltimore, Maryland. Hers was an idyllic family that was close-knit and enjoyed activities together. Seventeen years later, in 1966, when the young lady was about to enter her senior year of high school, she was on a summer outing to the beach. The girl dove into shallow water and injured her spine between the 4th and 5th vertebrae. The accident left the young lady paralyzed from the neck down. She began spinning into a growing sense of despair and hopelessness as the function of her arms and legs did not return. Her friends moved on with their lives in high school then later to college. We'll return to the rest of her story later.

There was another person - this one a man - born in the mid 1930's. He was a college professor who married and had two daughters. In the early

1970's, not too long after the previously mentioned young lady's accident, this man's youngest daughter was diagnosed with leukemia. She bravely battled the disease for a few years but finally succumbed when she was about six years old. The man was bitter at God and held onto that bitterness for the remaining 35 years of his life.

It is my conclusion (and the conclusion of nearly all who care to observe life) that everyone suffers. Some more than others, some more often than others, and some more publicly than others, but everyone suffers. A person's suffering might be physical, emotional, financial, relational, or spiritual.

Since everyone suffers, it might be wise to consider: how should I respond toward God during my suffering? How might I serve God in the tumultuous times I face? These are good questions to ponder and to come to conclusions about. We need look no further than the life of God's servant Job to get sage advice about how to serve God in the calamitous events and seasons of life.

Job is Described by his Master

The book of Job opens with some descriptive words regarding the man who is the main character of the book that bears his name. Job 1:1 states,

"There was a man in the land of Uz whose name was Job; and that man was blameless, upright, fearing God and turning away from evil."

Job's character is described before anything else is written about him. It is only later that his family and material wealth is mentioned and those only because they will play a significant part in his story. Have you ever noticed how rarely people's physical traits were mentioned in the Bible? The reason for this is that character matters far more than the person's size or appearance. God is far more interested in our character and it the development of our values.

We'll return to Job's character, as described by his Master, a bit later. Notice the following statements about Job:

The LORD said to Satan, "Have you considered My servant Job? For there is no one like him on the earth, a blameless and upright man, fearing God and turning away from evil."

The LORD said to Satan, "Have you considered My servant Job? For there is no one like him on the earth, a blameless and upright man fearing God and turning away from evil. And he still holds fast his integrity, although you incited Me against him to ruin him without cause." Job 1:8; 2:3

On those two occasions God described Job to Satan, that enemy of all of God's servants. Twice God referred to Job as "My servant" when speaking to Satan. You might remember that Lucifer, (his name as his creation as an angel of God), rebelled (Isaiah 14: 12-15; Ezekiel 28:14-19) and God changed his name to Satan, which means "adversary". Ever since, he has been the chief adversary of all - especially those who would follow God as obedient servants.

Much later in the book of Job, God described Job to his four friends who had harshly, verbally attacked Job's character. We read:

It came about after the LORD had spoken these words to Job, that the LORD said to Eliphaz the Temanite, "My wrath is kindled against you and against your two friends, because you have not spoken of Me what is right as My servant Job has. Now therefore, take for yourselves seven bulls and seven rams, and go to My servant Job, and offer up a burnt offering for yourselves, and My servant Job will pray for you. For I will accept him so that I may not do with you *according to your* folly, because you have not spoken of Me what is right, as My servant Job has (42:7, 8)."

Four times in those two verses, God referred to Job as "My servant" to Job's friends! Thus, we discover from chapters 1, 2, and 42 a total of six times this choice servant who suffered so much is referred to as God's servant. Perhaps God wants the reader to be absolutely clear what He thinks of Job!

Job's character is described

As mentioned previously, God refers to Job's character instead of his physical appearance or capabilities. God used four phrases in Job 1:1, 8 to describe his servant.

There was a man in the land of Uz whose name was Job; and that man was blameless, upright, fearing God and turning away from evil. The LORD said to Satan, "Have you considered My servant Job? For there is no one like him on the earth, a blameless and upright man, fearing God and turning away from evil."

- "No one like him or earth"

- "blameless"

- "upright"

- "fearing God and turning away from evil"

When the Master said there was "no one like him on earth", it was quite the compliment! To put it in modern vernacular, "he's one in a million." But truth be told, when we say that sort of thing we only know a limited number of people. I'd guess I know a few thousand people casually - enough to say I know them - but of many I have no idea about their true character. If I said that there was no one like him on earth, what I'm truly saying is he a rare guy unlike the other few thousand people I know casually. When God declares a person to be a one-of-a-kind, no-one-like-him sort of person, remember He know everything about everyone on earth. This was high praise!

Further God said of Job that he was "blameless". The King James Version (KJV) of the Bible translates the word as "perfect". That may be unintentionally misleading since we think the word "perfect" means without any fault or sin. The word means, "complete; entire; finished". When used as an adjective it meant "an absence of guile or deceit". Often at the Christmas holidays my family will purchase a 1,000-piece jigsaw puzzle and begin the task of putting it together. After many hours of work spread over several days, we finally complete it! I might add that one year my adult children left the last nearly 200 pieces for me to complete when they went to their homes. Those pieces were all zebra stripes that all looked the same! It took me days to compete. That's not a bad illustration of Job's life - he was like a completed jigsaw puzzle with no missing pieces and no glaring gaps in his character and personality.

Next God said of His servant that he was "upright". The word means "straight; level". That is, not crooked. With all due apologies to used car salesmen, Job was not a man who needed to call his business "Honest Job's Chariots". He was an upright guy who told the truth and was good for his word. If he shook your hand you didn't feel like you needed to go wash the grease off your hand. Job was the kind of man who would "level" with you.

He was a straight-shooter who spoke and lived honestly.

Lastly, of Job's character, God said he "feared God and turned away from evil." When one has a genuine fear of the holiness of God, she will also correspondingly turn away from evil. One of the major reasons our culture has plummeted so rapidly and deeply into sin is that most people, including many Christians, have lost any fear of God. Rather than turning from evil, most rush headlong after it.

If God were to describe you, would He do so with such complimentary terms? Is that what matter most to you - your character or your physical appearance and capabilities?

Job served his Master in the midst of his suffering

Job did not suffer then and only later serve his Master. He served while he suffered and did he suffer greatly! His was not a hang-nail, got-a-splinter-in-my hand sort of suffering. In Job's era, wealth was measured by the amount of livestock one owned, instead of the size of one's bank account. Job 1:2, 3 states:

> Seven sons and three daughters were born to him. His possessions also were 7,000 sheep, 3,000 camels, 500 yoke of oxen, 500 female donkeys, and very many servants; and that man was the greatest of all the men of the east.

You might be thinking, "I thought you said Job suffered greatly? Now you're telling me how rich he was." He was rich and knowing that gives us a greater appreciation of how much he lost, thus adding to his suffering. A person who's never had much doesn't have much to lose. Job had resources. He was the King Solomon of his day, or the Warren Buffett of the era.

So, what happened? Did he really lose that much? Look at what Job 1:13-19 says about his losses:

> Now on the day when his sons and his daughters were eating and drinking wine in their oldest brother's house, a messenger came to Job and said, "The oxen were plowing and the donkeys feeding beside them, and the Sabeans attacked and took them. They also slew the servants with the edge of the sword, and I alone have escaped to tell you." While he was still speaking, another also came and said, "The fire of God fell from heaven and burned up the sheep and the servants and consumed them, and I alone have escaped to tell you." While

he was still speaking, another also came and said, "The Chaldeans formed three bands and made a raid on the camels and took them and slew the servants with the edge of the sword, and I alone have escaped to tell you." While he was still speaking, another also came and said, "Your sons and your daughters were eating and drinking wine in their oldest brother's house, and behold, a great wind came from across the wilderness and struck the four corners of the house, and it fell on the young people and they died, and I alone have escaped to tell you."

To put his losses in perspective, he lost his savings account, his checking account, his piggy bank, and his pocket change. Even worse, all ten of his children died simultaneously. Imagine ten fresh graves all on the same day.

Lest you be tempted to think, "well at least Job still had his health," look at the next chapter. Job 2:1-8 says,

Again there was a day when the sons of God came to present themselves before the LORD, and Satan also came among them to present himself before the LORD. The LORD said to Satan, "Where have you come from?" Then Satan answered the LORD and said, "From roaming about on the earth and walking around on it." The LORD said to Satan, "Have you considered My servant Job? For there is no one like him on the earth, a blameless and upright man fearing God and turning away from evil. And he still holds fast his integrity, although you incited Me against him to ruin him without cause." Satan answered the LORD and said, "Skin for skin! Yes, all that a man has he will give for his life. However, put forth Your hand now, and touch his bone and his flesh; he will curse You to Your face." So the LORD said to Satan, "Behold, he is in your power, only spare his life." Then Satan went out from the presence of the LORD and smote Job with sore boils from the sole of his foot to the crown of his head. And he took a potsherd to scrape himself while he was sitting among the ashes.

God allowed Satan to afflict Job physically and he developed painful boils from head to toe. Further his wife was quite unsupportive and basically told Job, "if you curse God, He'll strike you dead." These incidents are prime examples of why most people associate Job with the concept of personal suffering.

How did Job respond? Consider what Job 1:20- 21 said, after he had lost all material possessions and all ten children:

Then Job arose and tore his robe and shaved his head, and he fell to the ground and worshiped. He said,

"Naked I came from my mother's womb,
And naked I shall return there.
The LORD gave and the LORD has taken away.
Blessed be the name of the LORD."

Job worshipped God amid his suffering. Worship is not necessarily a matter of posture,

103

though it may include kneeling, uplifted hands and gazing upward toward the heavens. It is more a matter of the heart, when the individual declares the greatness of God. In his excellent volume, *True Worship,* Warren Wiersbe writes, "Worship is a response of all that I am, body, soul, mind, emotion and will to all God is, says and does."

Worship is a choice we make. We either choose to do so or not. It is an overflow of the heart. A friend of mine used to say that when churches gather corporately to worship, the degree to which the individual members have worshipped during the other 166 hours of the week, will be the degree that corporate worship will occur when they are gathered. Put another way, we dare not think that when we gather that we can merely "flip a switch" and turn our worship on. Worship must have been a regular part of Job's life because it is evident it was his default setting during his storm.

As you think about your suffering and your worship, it might be helpful to understand that when Job responded to suffering with worship, he did

NOT know why his suffering was happening. He knew nothing of Satan's conversation with God nor of God's willingness to allow Satan to try Job. As someone once said, about trusting God in the midst of trouble when we have no idea why, "trust His (God's) heart even when you cannot see His hand."

Job guarded his words in his suffering
When - not if - we suffer we tend to complain, to accuse, to attack. We might direct this vitriol toward God or others or both. In the Exodus generation under Moses' leadership, there are ten occasions when the Bible records that they complained. When the apostle Peter faced potential suffering at the hands of Israel's leaders after Jesus was arrested, three times he denied he even knew who Jesus was. Perhaps that is why the Psalmist writes, "Set a guard, O Lord, over my mouth, keep watch over the door of my lips" (Psalm 141:3).

Jeremiah is often called "the weeping prophet" because of all the devastation he was forced to see. He wrote in his book of laments, we call it

Lamentations, "Why should any living mortal, or any man offer complaint in view of his sins?" (Lamentations 3:39). Job was very cautious with the God-given gift of speech. He did not slander or malign his Master even in his darkest hours.

All of us who have believed Jesus' offer of life eternal have not only been given life but also many other spiritual riches. We would be wise to ponder carefully before speaking rashly about God and harshly to others in our suffering. In your suffering, your greatest act of service might be seen in your words... or in your restraint of them.

Job understood the outcome of suffering

There are some short-term outcomes to suffering. These might include becoming more careful with one's words after having been falsely or harshly criticized. It might be that we develop boldness after suffering the guilt of denying Jesus as in Peter's case. Yes, there are many short-term outcomes to suffering. But I am convinced Job looked much further than a five-year plan - he looked down the hallways of time and eternity and said in Job 23:10

But He knows the away I take;
When He has tried me, I shall come forth as gold.

God is not capricious. He is not playing some sort of game with Job's life or yours. He is meticulously and wisely using every means, including all kinds of suffering, to refine and purify you just as a fiery furnace purifies gold. Centuries after Job's life, Peter's writes his first letter, using the theme of suffering and states,

In this you greatly rejoice, even though now for a little while, if necessary, you have been distressed by various trials, so that the proof of your faith, *being* more precious than gold which is perishable, even though tested by fire, may be found to result in praise and glory and honor at the revelation of Jesus Christ; (1Peter 1:6, 7).

Just as a surgeon might use a scalpel, a carpenter a hammer, and a baseball player a glove as their primary tools, to accomplish a task, God seems to use suffering as His key tool to renovate our values and character (see 2 Corinthians 4:16-

18). One significant problem we all have is the inability to see, and appreciate what God is doing, or where He is going with suffering. As I write these words I have two grandsons who are not quite 3 and 2 years old respectively. Both walk well and are even beginning to run. Long before that they each had to learn to crawl, stand, and then begin to take wobbly steps and both crashed dozens of times. I'm sure that, like their "papa", they did not appreciate the outcome of such suffering. It is only later that they - and we - can look back and see how the process of suffering nicks and bruises is required to become skilled walkers and runners. If we each understood those truths then, we might have been more patient in the process.

As you consider what you are currently suffering through and what you might be required to endure in the future, consider this: God is good all the time and He who gave His only Son for your justification is currently working to make you more like His son and prepare you for the kingdom.

Do you remember the young lady whose story we began this chapter with? You might have heard of her. She is Joni Erickson Tada. Joni has spent the past 50 years in a wheelchair. At the time of her accident, her suffering nearly overwhelmed her and it appeared any meaningful life she might live was over. But as God is prone to do, He has marvelously used Joni. She learned to paint beautifully holding a paint brush between her teeth. She founded a ministry called Joni & Friends which supplies wheelchairs for physically challenged people in third-world countries. I once attended a large gathering of pastors in a distant state. The key-note speakers were a veritable Who's Who of evangelical Christianity. One after the other they took turns speaking and challenging the several thousand pastors gathered. Then Joni rolled her wheelchair onto the stage. Her talk was riveting, more so than all who preceded and followed her. Why? Because God had refined her as gold through her suffering. Like Job of old, she has learned that one of her greatest opportunities to serve her Master has come through suffering.

When you consider God's servant Job, know this: his greatest service for his Master was possible due to his suffering and his response to it. Perhaps the same may be true of you too?

FOR FURTHER CONSIDERATION

1. Have you ever felt overwhelmed during times of suffering as Joni did after her accident?

2. What do you think was the major purpose for God allowing Job to suffer?

3. If God were to describe your character as He did Job's, what words would He use? Would He use words such as "blameless" and "upright"?

4. Have you noticed how careless we can be with our words toward God and others when we suffer?

5. In your suffering, will you pledge to consider the outcome of the suffering, not the specific details occurring in that moment?

Chapter 7

MY SERVANT, DAVID

Serving God from a position of authority

Who hasn't met a person in authority who started their career as the humble, happy-go-lucky sort? But as promotions came and the corporate ladder was climbed these people can become more and more surly. Regularly we hear about entertainers who begin their careers with a bit part in a movie later ascend to stardom and then become prima donnas.

Several years ago, an NBA player, who had begun his career in obscurity later became a star. After rising to stardom, he assaulted his coach and famously held out for a bigger contract. He stated his current multi-million-dollar per year contract was not enough and even said, "I have a family to feed too!"

It is not uncommon for ministry leaders to enter ministry to serve, experience the blessings of God and a measure of human success only to later become demanding and often a demeaning person toward other staff members and the flock under their care.

There is one servant, on God's brief list of "My servants" who did not fit this pattern, however. His name is David. He is one of the best-known characters of the entire Bible. His life, like all of God's servants, can teach us a great deal, especially regarding serving God from a position of prominence.

In case the Bible is a bit new to you, let's rehearse a little of this servant's background. He was a young man when Israel's first king, Saul, was in authority. God rejected Saul as king due to his rebellious heart, though he continued to reign for many more years. God instructed His prophet Samuel to anoint the next king of Israel. He instructed Samuel specifically to anoint a son of a man named Jesse. Jesse had eight sons with David being the youngest of them all.

As Samuel looked at Jesse's oldest son, Eliab, he hastily concluded, "that's the one God had chosen!" Why was Samuel so drawn to Eliab? He was tall, much like Saul. What a terrible reason to choose a king and leader. Nothing against tall people, but height doesn't make a good leader.

After being told "No" by God with the presentation of each of Jesse's older sons, Samuel asked, "Do you have any other sons?" Jesse said, in effect, "Yes, but he's the youngest, so we just left him out watching the sheep." In other words, "Samuel, you're wasting our time, he's not kingly material." Imagine your own father thinking so little of you that he didn't bother to have you come before the prophet to even be considered as Israel's second king.

David was anointed that day by Samuel as God's choice, though he would not become king for many more years. God told Samuel that while people look at the external characteristics, God looks at the heart (1 Samuel 16:7). As a song from years ago stated it, "While some men see a shepherd boy, God may see a king." Though anointed as king, David spent the better part of a decade fleeing Saul's murderous attempts on his life. At age thirty, after Saul was killed in battle, David finally was installed as Israel's second king.

David was strengthened by God and given victory after victory over Israel's enemies. In fact, the Bible informs us, "Now it came about when the king lived in his house, and the Lord had given him rest on every side from all his enemies..." (2 Samuel 7:1). The picture that comes to mind is that feeling one gets after an arduous task is completed, a lengthy and taxing "to do" list is all done, and you sit down with an "Ahhh!" That was the place David was in at that time in his life. He's king! He's wildly adored by the masses (the women sang, "Saul has killed his thousands but David his tens of thousands", 1 Samuel 18:7). He's been victorious in every battle. The kingdom has expanded greatly in size, and there is peace on every front!

David's plan to honor God

With peace, rest, and a life-is-good sort of mindset, David surveys his surrounding and draws a conclusion. 2 Samuel 7:2 tells us:

that the king said to Nathan the prophet, "See now, I dwell in a house of cedar, but the ark of God dwells within tent curtains."

Essentially David saw his magnificent house and compared it to God's "house" which, at this point, was the tabernacle - a portable tent that had been constructed during Moses' era. Sure, it was a nice tent, but it was a tent nonetheless. David thought it was not appropriate for God to not have a nicer "home". He determined he would do something to change the current situation and declared his plan to Nathan, God's prophet.

Certainly, David's heart was pure before God. It appears his driving motivation was to honor the One who had been so gracious to him. What gracious acts has God performed in you and for you? As you review God's blessings toward you, is your heart moved to honor Him? David's certainly was. What a great lesson to learn - a servant of God should always want to honor God. Our honoring God might take the form of generous giving to ministries God has raised up and that are true to His Word. It might be in heartfelt worship. It may take the form of forgiving a wrong suffered despite no apology or admission of wrong from the offender.

God says "No" to David's plan

As we have seen, David told Nathan the prophet of his intentions to build God a suitable house befitting His glory. Nathan immediately responded with "Great! Go ahead with the plan" (2 Samuel 7:3). That very night, God came to Nathan in a dream, saying:

But in the same night the word of the LORD came to Nathan, saying, "Go and say to My servant David, 'Thus says the LORD, "Are you the one who should build Me a house to dwell in? For I have not dwelt in a house since the day I brought up the sons of Israel from Egypt, even to this day; but I have been moving about in a tent, even in a tabernacle. Wherever I have gone with all the sons of Israel, did I speak a word with one of the tribes of Israel, which I commanded to shepherd My people Israel, saying, 'Why have you not built Me a house of cedar?'"' "Now therefore, thus you shall say to My servant David, 'Thus says the LORD of hosts, "I took you from the pasture, from following the sheep, to be ruler over My people Israel. I have been with you wherever you have gone and have cut off all your enemies from before you; and I will make you a great name, like the names of the great men who are on the earth. I will also appoint a place for My people Israel and will plant them, that they may live in their own place and not be disturbed again, nor will the wicked afflict them any more as formerly, even from the day that I commanded judges to be over My people Israel; and I will give you rest from all your enemies. The LORD also declares to you that the LORD will make a house for you. When your days are complete and you lie down with your fathers, I will raise up your descendant after you, who will come forth from you, and I will establish his kingdom. He shall build a house for My name, and I will establish the throne of his kingdom forever. I will be a father to him and he will be a son to Me; when he commits iniquity, I will correct him with the rod of men and the strokes of the sons of men, but My lovingkindness shall not depart from him, as I took *it* away from Saul, whom I removed from before you. Your house and your kingdom shall endure before Me forever; your throne shall be established forever."" In accordance with all these words and all this vision, so Nathan spoke to David (2 Samuel 7:4-17).

Through Nathan, God told David several things which included the concept of "no". No, David, I will not let you build the house you had intended to build. What a disappointing message that must have been! Elsewhere in scripture, we learn why God said no to David. It was because David was a warrior-king and God did not want His house, the temple, to be associated with bloodshed but peace

119

(1 Chronicles 22:8). Unlike David's experience here, sometimes God says no and gives no explanation as to why. Perhaps you've prayed for God to work in a certain way in you and through your life and He does not. Based upon circumstances, He seems to say no loud and clear.

Has God in recent days given you a "no" to some plans you've made? Perhaps they were even plans that were conceived due to a desire to please Him. One mark of maturity is how a person responds to frustrated plans. This principle is seen regularly when we observe people. Toddlers are famous for throwing tantrums when told "no" by their parents or others. A sure sign of progress in the maturation process is when they refuse to respond that way to a denial of plans.

God promises to bless His servant

God graciously did not merely say no to David and end His message. After issuing the "no" He also conveyed several promises and reminders to

His servant David. We read of them in 2 Samuel
7:5-16,

Go and say to My servant David, 'Thus says the LORD, "Are
you the one who should build Me a house to dwell in? For I
have not dwelt in a house since the day I brought up the sons
of Israel from Egypt, even to this day; but I have been moving
about in a tent, even in a tabernacle. Wherever I have gone
with all the sons of Israel, did I speak a word with one of the
tribes of Israel, which I commanded to shepherd My people
Israel, saying, 'Why have you not built Me a house of
cedar?'"' "Now therefore, thus you shall say to My servant
David, 'Thus says the LORD of hosts, "I took you from the
pasture, from following the sheep, to be ruler over My people
Israel. I have been with you wherever you have gone and have
cut off all your enemies from before you; and I will make you
a great name, like the names of the great men who are on the
earth. I will also appoint a place for My people Israel and will
plant them, that they may live in their own place and not be
disturbed again, nor will the wicked afflict them any more as
formerly, even from the day that I commanded judges to be
over My people Israel; and I will give you rest from all your
enemies. The LORD also declares to you that the LORD will
make a house for you. When your days are complete and
you lie down with your fathers, I will raise up
your descendant after you, who will come forth from you, and
I will establish his kingdom. He shall build a house for My
name, and I will establish the throne of his kingdom forever. I
will be a father to him and he will be a son to Me; when he
commits iniquity, I will correct him with the rod of men and
the strokes of the sons of men, but My lovingkindness shall
not depart from him, as I took *it* away from Saul, whom I
removed from before you. Your house and your kingdom
shall endure before Me forever; your throne shall be
established forever."'"

God reminds David of some truths and makes some wonderful promises to His servant. He reminded David of how far he had come from the sheepfold to the palace (verse 8). When David was younger he was left to watch his father's sheep while his seven older brothers auditioned before Samuel for the privilege to be king. Now he is king over God's people, a nation of nearly three million! Talk about a rags-to-riches story - this was one.

Further, God promised to give David victory over his enemies and make his name great (verse 9). God had already given David many victories (2 Samuel 7:1) and now promised to continue those successes. He also promised to make David's name great. He certainly has fulfilled that promise. To this day in Judaism, David is considered Israel's greatest king. His name and life are recorded throughout the Old and New Testaments. Millions of boys have been named David since then. Leonardo da Vinci masterfully sculpted an image of him. Others have painted scenes of his life. Yes, David's name has been made great.

In one sense, the greatest promise of all in this passage is found in verse 16, "And your house and your kingdom shall endure before Me forever; your throne shall be established forever". David's *house* and David's *throne* are equated in the promise. David had wanted to build God a house (a temple) yet God had said no. Here He promised David, "rather than you build me a house, I will build a house for you." The house God promised to build was not one of stone, wood, or marble but a house as used of royalty - a dynasty of kings (as we might say the House of Tudor or the House of Windsor when referring to England's royalty). David would have descendants to rule after him and this would continue forever!

The fulfillment of this promise will ultimately be Jesus Christ. In the gospel of Matthew, He is often referred to as the "Son of David". At other times, it was said of Him, "where is He who has been for king of the Jews, we have come to worship Him?" (Matthew 2:2). One day, perhaps soon, Jesus will sit upon a throne in Jerusalem to rule and reign forever (Isaiah 2:2-4; 9:6, 7; 11:1-5 and Revelation 22:1-3).

Imagine knowing that one of your great, great grandsons would be the long-promised Messiah and the eternal King!! Yes, God had said no to David, but He also said yes to some great and eternal promises. We'll return to this thought later in chapter 9; for now, know this: God always takes care of His servants. At times, His provision and care occur in this life. It will universally occur in the age to come.

David's response to his Master

To fully appreciate David's response, remember he's the same man who killed a lion and a bear that attacked his father's sheep. He's the same man who slew the giant, Goliath. He had a hit song sung about him by Israel's female choir (picture the female fans when the Beatles came to the United States). He's been victorious in every battle he's ever been in and his men greatly respect him and even risk their lives to serve him. He was once a lowly shepherd of a tiny flock, but now he's the king of a great nation. That's incredible stuff... the sort of stuff that usually goes to one's head. People like that - who've had a meteoric rise to fame and power - don't usually hear the word no or get denied any of their wishes. Yet David had been told no by God. How would he respond? Would he behave like an immature toddler and throw a tantrum or as a mature follower of God? We're not left to speculate as 2 Samuel 7 records his response.

David responded with such refreshing class it causes me to smile as I write these words. He didn't furrow his brow, or lash out at God with his words. He remained a humble servant throughout. 2 Samuel 7:18-29 states,

Then David the king went in and sat before the LORD, and he said, "Who am I, O Lord GOD, and what is my house, that You have brought me this far? And yet this was insignificant in Your eyes, O Lord GOD, for You have spoken also of the house of Your servant concerning the distant future. And this is the custom of man, O Lord GOD. Again what more can David say to You? For You know Your servant, O Lord GOD! For the sake of Your word, and according to Your own heart, You have done all this greatness to let Your servant know. For this reason You are great, O Lord GOD; for there is none like You, and there is no God besides You, according to all that we have heard with our ears. And what one nation on the earth is like Your people Israel, whom God went to redeem for Himself as a people and to make a name for Himself, and to do a great thing for You and awesome things for Your land, before Your people whom You have redeemed for Yourself from Egypt, *from* nations and their gods? For You have established for Yourself Your people Israel as Your own people forever, and You, O LORD, have become their God. Now therefore, O LORD God, the word that You have spoken concerning Your servant and his house, confirm *it* forever, and do as You have spoken, that Your name may be magnified forever, by saying, 'The LORD of hosts is God over Israel'; and may the house of Your servant David be established before You. For You, O LORD of hosts, the God of Israel, have made a revelation to Your servant, saying, 'I will build you a house'; therefore Your servant has found courage to pray this prayer to You. Now, O Lord GOD, You are God, and Your words are truth, and You have promised this good thing to Your servant. Now therefore, may it please You to bless the house of Your servant, that it may continue forever before You. For You, O Lord GOD, have spoken; and with Your blessing may the house of Your servant be blessed forever."

Rather than proudly believe God's gracious promises were deserved, David responds with, "Who am I, O Lord God, and what is my house, that Thou hast brought me this far?" David never lost his humility. He recognized it was the hand of a gracious God that had accomplished what had happened to bring him from the sheepfold to the palace. Further it was God's grace to promise a dynasty of kings to come through David's family tree.

Another response of David worth noting was his view of himself. Nine times in these verses David refers to himself as "Thy servant" or "Your servant". Over and over David, though a king, continues to repeat, "Lord I am still and ever your servant." How rare is that attitude since sin entered human history. Our natural tendency is toward pride and arrogance. We love being served and as we rise in position and rank, it becomes more and more common to be served and be able to expect - even demand - for others to serve us. As mentioned in chapter 1 regarding Pareto's Principle, 80% of all people in the average church have no position of regular service to others and the Lord. I don't know of any formal statistics that would prove it, but I'm relatively sure that the more power and prestige a person has, the less likely it becomes for her to view herself as a servant. Of the short list of God's servants in the Bible, only one was a king.

When you think of your relationship with Jesus, do you think of yourself as a servant or, as is so common these days and part of our nature, do you view God as your servant? David saw himself as God's servant when he was a young shepherd as well as when he was a powerful king.

If the Lord allows you to advance in your career and titles and accolades come, may you always view yourself as God's servant.

FOR FURTHER CONSIDERATION

1. Do you recall a time when a position or promotion went to your head and you acted more like a prima donna than a servant?

2. Do you recall a time when you were told no and you didn't understand but later learned a valuable lesson from the denial?

3. What do you think it would have been like for David to know his descendant would be the Messiah and rule forever?

4. In your relationship with God, one is the Master and the other the servant. Most often do you view God as the Master to be served, or the servant to meet your needs? Is that what God wants?

Chapter 8

My Servant, Isaiah

The servant who volunteered

Early in the 1940's the world was at war, especially in Europe. The United States had essentially kept a cool distance from entering the fray, even declining to assist long-time ally, England. Then the unthinkable happened. The Japanese attacked the United States at Pearl Harbor on December 7, 1941, resulting in the death of nearly 2,000 soldiers. In response, the U.S. officially entered the war. Another result was the overwhelming number of young men and women who volunteered to serve this great country and preserve its freedoms.

Not quite 70 years later, on September 11, 2001 there were terrorist attacks on the World Trade Center, the Pentagon, and a plane that eventually crashed in rural Pennsylvania killing more than

3,000 people. In response, thousands of young men and women – patriots - volunteered to serve this country. Among them was a notable volunteer named Patrick Daniel Tillman. Pat was born November 6, 1976 in Fremont, California. He starred as a football player at Arizona State University. Drafted in 1998 by the NFL Arizona Cardinals, he became a star. He was named to *Sports Illustrated's* All-Pro Team in 2000. After the September 11th attacks, Tillman completed the 2001 football season. In May of 2002, eight months after the incident, he enlisted in the U.S. Army, turning down a contract offer of $3.6 million dollars over the next three years. Tragically, Tillman was killed on April 22, 2004 by "friendly fire". His volunteer spirit and willingness to forgo a lucrative career to serve the United States remains an example for many.

What lead thousands in each of those two different generations to volunteer? I think it was that on both occasions they felt they had a cause worth fighting for, yes even dying for if need be.

As mentioned previously, in recent history it has been discovered that 80% of those who identify themselves as Christians have refused to volunteer for any meaningful service for Christ. This refusal or hesitancy to volunteer is nothing new. Do you remember when God called Moses to lead His people? If you read his story, as recorded in Exodus chapters 3 & 4, you will observe he offered excuses to God at least four times! God refused to accept any of them and countered them all with revelation about Himself and promises to Moses.

Why is it that so many hesitate to offer themselves up for service? Perhaps it is because they lack a compelling vision, an irresistible sense of obligation like so many young men and women had after the attacks at Pearl Harbor and on September 11, 2001.

There was a servant of God who readily volunteered and his story is instructive to all who wish to be servants of God. His name is Isaiah and his life's story is recorded in the Old Testament book that bears his name.

Before considering his life, we would do well to learn a bit about his era. Isaiah's name means "Yahweh saves". His life and ministry were lived out in the 8th century before Jesus. He was a prophet to the nation of Judah before her exile into Babylon. Judah, you might remember, was comprised of the southern two tribes of Israel after her split from the northern ten tribes, the result of the nation's civil war. Isaiah's life and ministry were carried out about the mid-point between Moses (15th century BC) and Jesus' incarnation and ministry.

Isaiah volunteered during chaotic times

Not unlike the World War II volunteers or the 9/11 volunteers, Isaiah's volunteerism did not occur in a vacuum. We read of his days in Isaiah 6:1, 9:

In the year of King Uzziah's death I saw the Lord sitting on a throne, lofty and exalted, with the train of His robe filling the temple. He said, "Go, and tell this people: 'Keep on listening, but do not perceive; Keep on looking, but do not understand.'

King Uzziah, who had been one of the longest reigning kings in Judah's history. He had ruled for 52 years and had recently died. He was a mostly good king (though pride led to leprosy as a judgment from God near the end of his life). So, one can imagine the angst many would have naturally felt; who would be the next king and what sort of king would he prove to be? To put the scene into perspective, imagine a president of the United States serving from the assassination of John F. Kennedy until the last year of the second term of Barrack H. Obama! That was how long Uzziah had been reigning and now the throne was empty.

Not only was there political uncertainty, there were spiritual problems galore. Isaiah 6:9 tells us that the people were spiritually deaf and blind. Earlier in Isaiah 1:2-4 the reader is informed:

Listen, O heavens, and hear, O earth; For the LORD speaks, "Sons I have reared and brought up, but they have revolted against Me. "An ox knows its owner, and a donkey its master's manger, *but* Israel does not know, My people do not understand." Alas, sinful nation, people weighed down with iniquity, Offspring of evildoers, sons who act corruptly! They have abandoned the LORD, they have despised the Holy One of Israel, they have turned away from Him.

A few chapters later Isaiah records the following:

Woe to those who add house to house *and* join field to field, Until there is no more room, so that you have to live alone in the midst of the land! Woe to those who rise early in the morning that they may pursue strong drink... Who stay up late in the evening that wine may inflame them! Woe to those who call evil good, and good evil; Who substitute darkness for light and light for darkness; Who substitute bitter for sweet and sweet for bitter! Woe to those who are heroes in drinking wine and valiant men in mixing strong drink... (Isaiah 5:8, 11, 20, 22).

To put it bluntly, Isaiah's culture was a spiritual mess. Lest we wag our fingers at those folks, recall that in recent days videos have surfaced of Planned Parenthood personnel offering to sell aborted baby body parts. Our culture no longer knows what the word marriage means. One's birth gender means little since one can change genders or decide to identify as either one depending on the day of the week or one's current emotions and state of mind. When it comes to values, we tend to be very materialistic rather than generous toward others with God-given resources.

Our culture is in as much need - if not more - as Isaiah's culture. Stated another way, your service for God is desperately needed. Do you see the needs that exist or do you see only the mess people have made of their lives?

Isaiah volunteered because of God's majesty

Isaiah's volunteerism did not merely occur during some chaotic times, it also was the result of getting a clear glimpse of the One whom he would serve, should he volunteer. Isaiah 6:1-4 states:

In the year of King Uzziah's death I saw the Lord sitting on a throne, lofty and exalted, with the train of His robe filling the temple. Seraphim stood above Him, each having six wings: with two he covered his face, and with two he covered his feet, and with two he flew. And one called out to another and said, "Holy, Holy, Holy, is the LORD of hosts, the whole earth is full of His glory." And the foundations of the thresholds trembled at the voice of him who called out, while the temple was filling with smoke.

In his vision, Isaiah saw God seated on a throne. Not only was He seated on a throne, but He was lofty and exalted. The kingdom of Judah, long reigned over by Uzziah, may have had a recently vacated throne but the throne of heaven had Someone still occupying it!

It's one thing to have a vacancy on the throne. It's quite another to have the throne occupied by a person whose character is unbecoming. Such was NOT the case in Isaiah's vision. Not only was the throne occupied by God, the angelic host declared of Him, "Holy, holy, holy…" The word holy means "pure, righteous; absence of any impurity". Many have suggested, and rightly so, that holiness is the central character trait or attribute of God. It is the only one of all His attributes that is mentioned three times consecutively. Aren't you glad the throne of the universe is occupied by an absolutely holy God? If He weren't holy He could use His power evilly. If He were not holy, He could use His exhaustive knowledge evilly too.

Many people see God not as a holy, exalted, sovereign king but as a Santa who should give them everything on their wish list; or as an old man who is gentle but rather inept; or as a boss who gives commands but no one really has to listen to Him or obey Him.

What is your view of God? It will largely determine if you serve Him and if so how faithfully you do so.

Do you remember the twelve men Jesus called to follow Him as disciples? They each saw His majesty on many occasions. After the resurrection (except for Judas) they all served Him. According to church tradition, ten of the eleven died as martyrs. John was the lone exception and he was exiled to the Island of Patmos due to his service for Christ. Majesty has a way of changing people.

I recall an old poem we used to read to our children when they were younger, it went as follows:

Pussy cat, pussy cat, where have you been?
I've been to London to see the queen.
Pussy cat, pussy cat, what did you there?
I saw a mouse under her chair.

Cats have the tendency to see mice even when in the presence of royalty. So, the proverbial cat missed the majestic scene of the throne room because its focus was all wrong. Like the cat in the presence of the queen, we too can focus on all the wrong things. Rather than mice, we might focus on other's mistakes, possessions we'd like to have, the opinions of others, and more. If we, like Isaiah, truly get a sense of the majesty and holiness of our

God, we will be moved to volunteer - to serve. Chances are good you won't have a vision of God's holiness as vivid as was Isaiah's. How then can you get a glimpse of His holiness? You'll get a better glimpse of His perfection and holiness through a regular intake of God's Word. As you read thoughtfully and meditate on it carefully, you will sense the grandeur of God.

Isaiah volunteered as a cleansed servant

Isaiah's culture was filled with political uncertainty and spiritual anemia. It would have been easy for him not to volunteer to serve God or volunteer with lots of personal baggage. Before he volunteered, he took care of some personal spiritual issues. Isaiah 6:5-7 records:

Then I said, "Woe is me, for I am ruined! Because I am a man of unclean lips, and I live among a people of unclean lips; For my eyes have seen the King, the LORD of hosts." Then one of the seraphim flew to me with a burning coal in his hand, which he had taken from the altar with tongs. He touched my mouth *with it* and said, "Behold, this has touched your lips; and your iniquity is taken away and your sin is forgiven."

When Isaiah witnessed the glory and holiness of God, he was confronted with his own need for

140

cleansing. Remember king Uzziah who had recently died (Isaiah 6:1)? He had died as a ceremonially unclean man because of leprosy. The nation of Judah was largely an unclean people as they pursued idolatry and many other sins. It is in view of those two realities that Isaiah proclaimed, "Lord, I am an unclean man!"

Often it is stated that God uses people who are available. While that is true, He also desires and most often uses people who are not clinging to known sin. He uses available *cleansed* people. A New Testament picture of a believer is that we are all clay pots. God uses all shapes and sizes of people for a variety of purposes, but He refuses to use dirty pots. Romans 12:1, 2 supports this truth when it says:

Therefore I urge you, brethren, by the mercies of God, to present your bodies a living and holy sacrifice, acceptable to God, *which is* your spiritual service of worship. And do not be conformed to this world, but be transformed by the renewing of your mind, so that you may prove what the will of God is, that which is good and acceptable and perfect.

So how does a dirty vessel become clean? How can the sacrifice of our lives become a holy one? I John 1:9, addressing the issue of sin in the life of the believer and its consequent loss of fellowship says, "If we confess our sin, He is faithful and just to forgive us our sin and cleanse us from all unrighteousness."

In a word, the way to cleansing is "confession". To confess sin is a bit like a criminal who confesses, saying to the judge, "Your honor, I plead guilty. I did what I've have been charged with". The wonderful truth is that God promises to forgive the son or daughter who confesses his sin. When confession occurs, the child of God is restored to fellowship. Her standing before her heavenly Father is now a joyous one, rather than one marked by distance and rebellion.

God gave Isaiah a glimpse of His holiness and it drove Isaiah to confess his impurity. Someone has said, "God doesn't drive us to despair to leave us there, but to change us".

Have you ever worn a pair of fairly nice white tennis shoes to the store to try on a new pair of tennis shoes? I usually try on the new shoe on my right foot first. When I do this, the left shoe, which looked pretty good, now looks quite disgusting - like it should be washed with extra bleach. When we see God's holiness through His Word, the Bible, we are often compelled to see and confess our sin. Has the Holy Spirit recently shown you an impurity that doesn't reflect the Father's holiness? What will you do about it? If you have not yet confessed a known sin that He's clearly revealed, don't you think you ought to right now?

Isaiah volunteered unconditionally

It is important to understand when God asked, "whom shall I send and who will go for us?" He is NOT in need of help. Rather in grace He invites His sons and daughters to partner with Him in His work.

To use our terms, Isaiah raised his hand to volunteer. We read in Isaiah 6:8,

Then I heard the voice of the Lord, saying, "Whom shall I send, and who will go for Us?" Then I said, "Here am I. Send me!"

You will note that Isaiah did not say to God, "I'll only serve in a very specific capacity, but don't ask me to do anything else or different." Neither was his volunteerism conditioned by saying, "I'll do anything you want but _____."

Early in my ministry I essentially told God there were two things I would not do; 1) pastor a church (public speaking scared me to death) and 2) missions (missionaries always seemed to be asking for money for their ministry). In God's timing and with His sense of humor, I pastored a church for nearly 15 years and grew to love preaching. Later I worked in a Bible College setting where I regularly asked people to support our ministry!

Have you been struck with the grandeur and purity of God? To the extent to which you have is directly related to the extent you'll volunteer to serve.

What ministry vacancies exist at your church or a non-profit in your area? What ministry has God been prompting you to launch? Raise your hand, step up, and get going!

FOR FURTHER CONSIDERATION

1. Do our culture's problems cause you to retreat or to volunteer to make a change?

2. Can you recall a time you sensed the holiness of God as never before? How did you feel at that moment?

3. Have you ever volunteered but knowingly held on to some sin(s) in your life? How did that work out for you?

4. Have you ever volunteered so serve God, but with very specific conditions attached?

Chapter 9

God rewards His servants

Motivation for a lifetime of service

More years ago than I care to admit, I played Little League baseball. The year was 1967 and in my home town, Tulsa, Oklahoma, there were approximately 1500 second- graders like me playing baseball. The team I was on was quite good – so good in fact that we won our league and went to the playoffs. We kept winning all the way to the city championship game, which we lost. After the game, the players on the winning team were each presented a large trophy for 1st place. My teammates and I were each given a smaller 2nd place trophy. The remaining 1475, or so, 2nd grade boys did not receive a trophy. Essentially, they were told, "try again next year fellas".

Nearly thirty years later when my own children completed in sports, they all got a trophy merely for being on a team. They call them participation trophies. The problem with participation trophies is that they devalue all trophies, kids don't value something if everyone receives one.

Do the "My Servants" of this book receive the same reward or trophy as those prodigals who squander many years of life? Do the 20% of the Pareto Principle, who serve faithfully and give consistently and generously, receive the same reward as the 80% who have no ministry and rarely serve and inconsistently give?

Another very important question to ask and get answered is this, are the prizes/trophies at the end of life worth the effort it takes to win one? As a boy, I used to enjoy Cracker Jacks. For my younger readers, Cracker Jacks is toffee covered popcorn and peanuts packaged in a small box. On each box was a notice, "Prize Inside". Kids in my day used to beg their parents for money to buy a box of Cracker Jacks. When successful in obtaining money from mom or dad, we'd open the box and start eating the snack and digging for the prize. Every time it was a disappointment! The prizes were never good. I'm an optimist and kept thinking the next box I bought would have a good prize in it but it never did. Are God's prizes to His servants like those Cracker Jacks prizes, disappointing and underwhelming? Do those who serve Jesus faithfully have a disappointing prize to anticipate or what?

Stated briefly, not every believer in Christ will receive rewards yet those who do will NOT be sorry for the time and effort they put forth to receive them. Servants of Christ will be greatly rewarded for all their service for the King.

Motivation for rewards

Why would anyone be motivated to serve Jesus? Why do some seem to have little or no motivation to serve Him? While there may be many other good reasons to serve Jesus, some of them are:

- God's great love for us (Eph. 3:17-19).
- Our love for God (2 Cor. 5:14).
- Our deep sense of how much we've been forgiven (Luke 7:47)
- To please Jesus (2 Cor. 5:9).

Yet there is another motivation mentioned often in the New Testament, namely the possibility of receiving rewards from Jesus at the Judgement Seat of Christ. In fact, it is the leading motivation used in the New Testament considering how many times this motivation is employed.

It is important to keep in mind, though, that one can have more than one motivation for service. I might serve out of great love for Christ, as a thank you for my sense of how much I've been forgiven, and because of the rewards He's promised in His Word. I played baseball because I love the game, I am competitive, and I wanted to win a trophy.

Lest you think I inflate the prominence of rewards out of proper proportion, consider the following:

- The apostle Paul declared his ambition in life was to receive rewards at the Judgment Seat of Christ (2 Cor. 5:8-10).
- Moses turned his back on the splendor of Egypt and identified with the enslaved

people of God because he was looking toward a reward (Hebrews 11:24-26)

- Jesus, in some of His last recorded words in the Bible, promised rewards to His followers according to their works. Revelation 22:12, "Behold I am coming quickly, and My reward is with Me, to render to every man according to what He has done."

Someday, perhaps soon, Jesus will return to rapture His church to heaven (1 Thessalonians 4:13-17). Soon after that occurrence the New Testament declares that each individual believer in Jesus will undergo an evaluation which is referred to as the Judgment Seat of Christ.

What is the Judgment Seat of Christ?

Sometimes it is helpful to discover what is NOT meant in defining terms or concepts. This is especially true of the Judgment Seat of Christ. It has nothing to do with *where* a person will spend eternity. Put another way, it is NOT to determine who goes to heaven and who goes to hell. That determination was made in life by an individual's response to the gospel. Only those who, by faith, responded to Jesus' offer of eternal life will be present at this event.

Unfortunately, when some people hear the words, "judgment seat" they think negative thoughts. I've had people say to me, "Bill, the Bible says that, in Jesus, all my sins have been judged and I won't have to face judgment for my sins". While that is true, the concept of the judgment seat is not one of condemnation but one of determination. A judge at an athletic competition doesn't condemn athletes, he pronounces winners and awards them prizes based upon their performance.

What will Jesus evaluate?

Jesus will evaluate the believer's service, her good works done from the moment of salvation until death or the rapture, whichever comes first. The works of service He evaluates may be minute or major – even a cup of water given to a thirsty person is a rewardable act.

Some wrongly conclude that only outstanding, noticeable by others, acts of service will be rewarded. They assume things like preaching, singing a solo, being a seminary professor and the like are major and other things like opening a door for an elderly person, helping a neighbor a project, and such are too ordinary to be rewarded. No, Jesus will reward EVERY good work ever done. Even the ones unnoticed by others and perhaps long forgotten by others and ourselves. Think of it, that may well include thousands upon thousands of deeds done. If He promised to reward giving a cup of water to a thirsty person and He took notice of a poor widow giving two small coins in an offering basket (Mark 12:41-44; Luke 21:1-4) He surely will notice what you've done in service for Him. What a great comfort! Personally, I know many who have gotten discouraged when thinking of how little they've done for Jesus, that day will be a good reminder of things done but long forgotten.

Jesus will not *merely* evaluate one's service, He will also evaluate one's motives behind the works (1 Corinthians 4:5). Matthew's gospel records Jesus' teaching His disciples as He warned them to avoid the examples of some religious leaders of that day. Jesus said that some prayed, gave gifts to the poor and even fasted (all good things) but only to be seen by people (Matthew 6:1-7). Good works? Yes, but unfortunately compelled by impure motives.

How, you might ask, can motives be evaluated? Who can "read" the motives behind a person's actions? Only God knows the motives of a person's heart. Jesus is God incarnate and He can read motives, 1 Corinthians 4:5 states:

Therefore do not go on passing judgment before the time, *but wait* until the Lord comes who will both bring to light the things hidden in the darkness and disclose the motives of *men's* hearts; and then each man's praise will come to him from God.

Did you notice that the Lord will disclose the motives of a person's heart? Others may misread my motives, but Jesus will not. That, like most truth can be a two-edged sword: When my motives are less than good, it is a dreadful thing, but when they are pure this truth brings great comfort.

Jesus will evaluate **what** we did (works of service) and **why** we did those things (motives that prompted the works). Ultimately, He will not be looking for perfection but faithfulness (1 Corinthians 4:2). None of us are perfect, and most of us are quite normal – we're not "stars". But we can all be faithful to plod along, take one step of obedience after another in our service for Jesus.

What rewards might Jesus give us?

Remember the Cracker Jacks prize? It was not worth the effort to dig it out of the bottom of the box. Will Jesus' prizes be worth the effort? Here are a few of the prizes the New Testament declares could be ours:

1. A Commendation from Jesus. This is, perhaps, the best-known prize. It may include the words, "well done, thou good and faithful servant" (Mt. 25:21). Can you imagine, after a careful examination of your entire life, Jesus commending you with words like that? "Great job, a life well lived!" Most of us know what it's like to undergo a performance evaluation at work. It's nice to hear a

boss say, "You did excellent work last year!"
Imagine the crucified Lamb and coming King
saying about your entire life, "Outstanding!"

2. A commission from Jesus. Though the
American political system is fraught with
imperfection, it does teach a lesson regarding
service. When a person is elected president, no
matter what political party he represents, he gives
positions to those who have been faithful to him.
These might include high level cabinet positions,
lower level ambassadorships, and so on. Similarly,
Jesus, when He rules all creation, will give
positions, responsibilities to His faithful servants
(Matthew 25:21- speaks of ruling over 10 cities;
Matthew 19:28 – speaks of some ruing over larger
groups of people). The principle is that when a
person has been faithful in little (the opportunities
God gave us in this brief life) Jesus will entrust to
her much greater responsibility in the kingdom to
come.

By-the-way, this is why crowns are mentioned
so often in the New Testament. Kings and queens

wear crowns – they are symbols of authority. One day the King of kings will delegate authority to some of His servants to rule under His authority. What a great privilege! The apostle Paul said it well when he said of athletes, they train to win crowns that fade (laurel wreaths placed upon the heads of champions) but believers should train to win crowns that will never fade (imperishable – 1 Corinthians 9:25). The crown we might receive and the positions that go with them will continue forever. In fact, Revelation 22, the last chapter in our Bibles, says that those who rule will rule forever (22:5).

Many other rewards are possible, including a new name from Jesus (Revelation 2:17); a personal commendation before the Father and holy angels (Revelation 3:5). Imagine Jesus giving you a new name, suited to your character and life, and bragging about you, "Father, angels, this is My faithful servant _____!"

Yes, the rewards offered really are worth the effort. His praise will be worth the effort, time, suffering, and disappointment endured to serve Him.

If you're a parent, you, no doubt, have had occasions to have your children make you very proud. They starred in a ball game, did wonderfully at a recital, or gave a great valedictory address. When children do those sorts of things, they make their parents look good. Similarly, when God's children serve Him faithfully and with pure motives, He is glorified.

The Father received abundant glory from the lives of His servants, Jesus, Abraham, Moses, Caleb, Job, David and Isaiah. Is He and will He from your life?

May you live in such a way that God cold say of you, "My Servant" and Jesus could say of you, "Well done, My servant! You lived life well and served me faithfully!"

FOR FURTHER CONSIDERATION

1. When you were growing up, were trophies rare or commonplace and how did this affect your view of them?

2. Can you recall a time when the prize you received was not worth the effort it took to get the prize?

3. How does knowing Jesus will evaluate your life one-day influence how you live today?

4. What do you think it would be like to hear Jesus brag about you and a life well lived?

About the author:

Bill Korver came to faith in Jesus Christ as a young boy and was raised in a Christ-centered home. He is a graduate of Southeastern Bible College (B.A. in Pastoral Theology and an M.A. in Biblical Studies), Luther Rice University (M. Div.) and Liberty University (D. Min.)

He served as a youth pastor (1982-1988), a church planter and pastor (1989-2004) and as president of Carolina College of Biblical Studies since 2004.

He is married to Marcia and together they have three adult children. He loves reading, teaching God's Word, working in the yard and hunting.

For questions or comments, Bill F. Korver can be reached at billfkorver@gmail.com

CPSIA information can be obtained
at www.ICGtesting.com
Printed in the USA
FSHW021701141019
63009FS